LAW OF THE LAND

A Practical Legal Guide for Tourists and Business Travelers

Japan

By Michael L. Moore Esq.

DEDICATION

This book is dedicated to the memory of my late older brother, Kenneth Lee Moore, whose tragic murder at 15 years of age inspired me to write this series of books.

This book is also dedicated to my parents, John Henry Moore, and Edna Mae Moore, whose tremendous parenting skills kept me focused on the important things in life: being reverent, getting educated, and prioritizing family.

Finally, this book is dedicated to my beautiful family, my wife Royellen, my son AJ, and my daughter Karla. They inspire me every single day to be kind, patient, and compassionate.

IN LOVING MEMORY OF:

Belinda Joyce Moore Moss—my beautiful and wonderful sister, who supported me in every positive thing that I ever attempted to do.

Michael Eugene Baker—my dedicated and loyal friend and brother, who always wanted the very best for me.

Sylvia Joyce Hill—my eldest sister, who had a beautiful spirit and was like a second mother to me.

LAW ⚖ OF THE LAND ®

PUBLISHING for Tourists & Business Travelers

Travel smart. Stay legal. Stay safe.®

From local laws to medical guides we've got you covered world wide
in one digital platform.

Travel Safe Anywhere
3 MONTHS FREE TRIAL

SCAN QR code
for more info

PREFACE

My introduction to the justice system came when I was only 10 years old. My 15-year-old brother was murdered with a butcher knife by a 19-year-old in a simple argument over a torn shirt. I was devastated by his death and sought retribution for his fate that never came. The woman was initially charged with second degree murder, but after plea negotiations, she was convicted of manslaughter and sentenced to only five years in a youthful offender school and ordered to undergo psychiatric care. That was it. Nothing more. The judicial system had run its course.

My family knew nothing about the justice system, and we did not have the tools to advocate for ourselves. No one provided us with a written source to reference for guidance through this process. There was no easily accessible, easy to understand, definitive source to educate ourselves about the legal system that we suddenly and unexpectedly found ourselves immersed in after being victimized by such a violent criminal act.

As I got older, finished college, law school, and ultimately started practicing law, it became clear to me that most people are not knowledgeable about the law or how the judicial process works. If most people are uninformed here in the United States regarding the law and the legal process, how would they fare when in other countries? I realized that tourists and businesspeople who travel internationally needed access to information on how to navigate the legal system in other countries!

For many years, there has been considerable media attention focused on international travelers experiencing legal difficulties while traveling abroad. Most of these news stories gained attention in the United States and abroad because they involved American citizens facing punishment

5

that was considered "unconventional" and "harsh" by United States' legal standards. I recall a news story in 1994 regarding Michael Fay, a young American male, who had broken the law in Singapore. He was convicted and sentenced to be caned and or whipped publicly. While the United States Government weighed in on the inappropriate and cruel nature of the punishment, the young American was beaten because he had been convicted under Singapore law.

Similarly, in recent years, international news stories have garnered head-lines regarding foreign travelers and their issues with the laws of countries that were not their own. Amanda Knox, an American woman, was accused of murdering her roommate in Italy in 2007 and spent almost four years in an Italian prison before being definitively acquitted by the Supreme Court of Cassatio. Kenneth Bae, an American citizen, was arrested in North Korea in 2012 and was convicted for hostile acts against the communist country. He was sentenced to 15 years hard labor but was released in 2014 after efforts by the U.S. State Department. More recently, United States Basketball Star, Brittany Griner was arrested in February 2022 at a Moscow airport on drug-related charges and detained for nearly 10 months, spending much of that time in prison. Her plight unfolded at the same time Russia invaded Ukraine and further heightened tensions between Russia and the United States, ending only after she was freed in exchange for a notorious Russian arms dealer.

It was in 1994 that another personal tragic event occurred that finally inspired me to write these series of books. A dear friend and also client of mine was brutally murdered while on his second honeymoon in Jamaica. News of his murder shocked me and our local community. The legal hurdles his family had to overcome to see that justice was properly dispensed far away from home, in another country, with an entirely different set of criminal procedural rules and laws, was difficult to navigate.

As I was my friend's attorney at the time of his death, his family asked that I act as their "legal liaison" to the Jamaican Prosecutor's Office and to the Jamaican Police Department. I participated in multiple police interviews with my client's widow because she was the primary witness to his murder. As a former prosecuting attorney, I was also allowed by the Court, as a professional courtesy, to sit at the prosecutor's table to consult with the prosecuting attorney during trial. What I observed about the Jamaican trial process from a front row seat was compelling enough to cause me to seriously consider educating the "world" regarding what to expect and how to act appropriately when faced with legal issues while traveling abroad.

One of the realities in life is that, regardless of what country you are in, it is never a pleasant experience to run afoul of the law and be forced to accept that someone else will be making a decision about your pecuniary, proprietary, or penal interests (your money, your property, or your freedom).

It is important to know what the laws are, how they apply to you, and how to navigate the legal system if you are charged with a crime. It is also very helpful to know what resources are available to you if you are the victim of a criminal act. At the end of the day, an "ounce of prevention is worth a pound of cure," so the more knowledge you have, the more ammunition you possess, and the more likely you will have a positive outcome.

If you are traveling to Japan, the first thing you should pack is a copy of this book! The helpful information and tips contained in this volume will provide a great starting point for knowing what to do (and not to do!) when you arrive at your destination and will help ensure that you have a wonderful vacation or business trip unmarred by tangles with the law.

TABLE OF CONTENTS

INTRODUCTION

INTRODUCTION

As a practicing attorney for over 34 years, I have encountered numerous clients who travel often, but are unaware of the laws of the land they are traveling to.

Therefore, many years ago, I decided to write a series of books that would explain the laws of specific countries. My focus was to explain the laws that may affect travelers in a straightforward manner, without all of the legal language that is sometimes hard for even seasoned attorneys to understand.

About This Book

The aim of this book is simple. It provides you, the traveler, with a simple, easy to read book that will provide a basic legal guide that explains the law in the country that you are about to visit. It is not intended to educate you on ALL of the laws in a given country. The goal is to provide you with the details of the most common legal and safety issues faced by tourists and business travelers.

I have also provided context with background information on places not to visit, statistics on the country and prevention measures you should take to safeguard your legal and physical safety. Knowledge is a powerful thing and knowing how to stay out of trouble (or how to get out of it!) is important for everyone who travels.

This *Law of The Land/Japan* book simply helps you become more informed about your legal rights, responsibilities, and obligations in a wide range of subject areas.

Last, but not least, this book does NOT purport to offer legal advice. It does, however, provide the information you need to stay safe, follow the law and navigate around legal difficulties. However, if you do face legal difficulties, the information in this book will provide you with a starting point for solving the problem and obtaining legal assistance should it be required.

Hypotheticals Used Throughout This Book

From time to time throughout this book, I will explain the law to readers by using hypothetical scenarios. These hypotheticals will be marked by an icon that will be explained in further detail as you read on.

How This Book is Organized

CHAPTER 1: **About Japan.** This chapter will provide you with a brief overview about Japan and its history. It also addresses Visa requirements, monetary advice, and the best times to visit.

CHAPTER 2: **Customs.** This chapter will provide information on what to expect when entering Japan. It will also explain what restricted and prohibited items are when entering Japan along with custom's regulations.

CHAPTER 3: **Crime in Japan.** This chapter provides an overview of the history of crime in Japan and steps that Japan's officials have taken to curb the high rate of crime.

CHAPTER 4: **Criminal Law Violations.** This chapter will provide information on drug offenses, penalties, true events and questions and answers.

CHAPTER 5: **Alcohol-Related Offenses.** This chapter will provide key points regarding the sale, consumption, and regulations of alcohol use in Japan.

CHAPTER 6: **Firearm & Ammunition Offenses.** This chapter will provide key points regarding the possession of firearms and ammunition in Japan.

CHAPTER 7: **Prostitution.** This chapter provides an overview of the history of prostitution in Japan, laws and penalties, prostitution practices, sex trafficking, sex tourism, health in Japan, tips to avoid being hassled, a Law of the Land Hypothetical, and the current situation on prostitution in Japan.

CHAPTER 8: **LGBTQ.** This chapter will provide information regarding the acceptance of LGBTQ people in Japan and the laws surrounding homosexuality.

CHAPTER 9: **Sexually Motivated/Violent Crimes.** This chapter will provide an overview of sexually related crimes in Japan.

CHAPTER 10: **Arrested in Japan.** This chapter will provide information on what to do if you are arrested in Japan.

CHAPTER 11: **Jails vs. Prisons: Conditions & Culture.** This chapter will provide information on the conditions and culture of Japan's Jails and Prisons.

CHAPTER 12: **Helping a Friend or Relative Imprisoned in Japan.** This chapter will provide information on how you can assist a friend or relative imprisoned in Japan.

CHAPTER 13: **The Administration of Justice.** This chapter will provide information on Japan's Legal System.

CHAPTER 14: **Crime Victim Assistance.** This chapter will provide information on crime victim assistance along with providing safety tips.

CHAPTER 15: **Police.** This chapter will provide information on Japan's Police and how to report a crime.

CHAPTER 16: **How to Get Legal Help in Japan.** This chapter will provide information regarding how to obtain legal assistance for travelers to Japan.

CHAPTER 17: **Medical Facilities & Hospitals.** This chapter will provide information about how to obtain medical care while visiting Japan.

CHAPTER 18: **Driving in Japan.** This chapter will provide information on driving in Japan, it's traffic rules, and road safety tips.

CHAPTER 19: **Nude Beaches & Clothing-Optional Resorts.** This chapter will provide an overview of nude beaches and clothing-optional resorts in Japan, and the legality and safety of visiting nude beaches in Japan.

CHAPTER 20: **Unusual Laws.** This chapter will provide information on some Unusual Laws in Japan, and penalties and fines.

CHAPTER 21: **Traveling Safely.** This chapter will provide information on women traveling alone, crime prevention for families, safety notes for all travelers, and overall advice.

CHAPTER 22: **Tourist Taxation.** This chapter will provide information on taxes that tourists are required to pay in Japan.

CHAPTER 23: **Long-Term Stays.** This chapter will provide an overview of the consequences for overstaying your visit to Japan.

CHAPTER 24: **Civil Litigation.** This chapter will provide information about the civil litigation process in Japan.

CHAPTER 25: **Other Things to Know.** This chapter will provide information on the harassment of tourists, travel and safety, and other practical tips.

CHAPTER 26: **Quick Reference Guide.** This chapter is a quick way to get information. It is a condensed version of the chapters in this book.

Emergency/Important Contact Numbers in Japan

Useful Japanese Phrases

Glossary

Icons Used in this Book

What do those pictures throughout the book mean? See below:

WARNING: This icon flags information about things you should **avoid** while visiting Japan. Heed the advice next to this icon to avoid legal perils.

REMEMBER: This icon flags noteworthy information that you **shouldn't forget.**

HELPFUL TIPS: This icon flags information that will help you when entering Japan, relates to a legal situation, or refers to resources available while visiting Japan.

TECHNICAL INFORMATION: This icon flags technical aspects of the law. If you are faced with a legal problem, and you want to learn more about the law involved, this information can be helpful.

 **ADDITIONAL INFORMATION**: This icon points to the location of additional information available on the internet.

 **HYPOTHETICAL**: This icon points to hypothetical scenarios to illustrate possible legal problems and the outcome.

 **QUESTIONS**: This icon points to questions and answers throughout the book.

 **TRUE STORY**: This icon points to true events throughout the book.

Where to Go From Here

If you have a specific question about the law in Japan as it relates to a particular area, just turn to the chapter that addresses that issue, or turn to the Quick Reference Guide. You can also read the book from cover to cover to obtain a more comprehensive understanding of the Japanese laws and resources available should you find yourself in a legal predicament while visiting.

 **Disclaimer:** While the recommendations in this book primarily address U.S. citizens, the information is relevant and applicable to citizens of any country.

ABOUT JAPAN

CHAPTER 1
ABOUT JAPAN

About Japan

Japan is an island nation located in **East Asia**, situated in the Pacific Ocean. It consists of **four main islands**—Honshu, Hokkaido, Kyushu, and Shikoku—along with many smaller islands. Covering an area of about **145,937 sq miles**, it is roughly the size of Germany or the state of California but is far more mountainous and densely populated. With a **population** of **around 125 million people**, Japan is one of the most densely populated countries in the world, particularly in its major cities like Tokyo, Osaka, and Kyoto.

Known for its rich cultural heritage, Japan blends ancient traditions with modern influences. It is famous for its tea ceremonies, sumo wrestling, and calligraphy, as well as its global pop culture impact, especially in anime, manga, and video games. Japan is a leader in technological innovation, especially in electronics, robotics, and automotive industries. The country's natural beauty, from Mount Fuji to its hot springs and cherry blossoms, adds to its worldwide allure. Its cuisine, including sushi, ramen, and sashimi, has also become internationally loved.[1]

Japan's history stretches back thousands of years, starting with the Jomon people, who arrived around **14,000 BCE**. The country later developed a distinct cultural identity, influenced by Buddhism and China.

---

1   https://www.britannica.com/place/Japan

The classical period saw the rise of the samurai class, and Japan's capital moved to **Kyoto**. By the 12th century, Japan became a **feudal society** dominated by military leaders known as **shoguns**. The Tokugawa Shogunate ushered in the Edo period, a time of peace and isolation, lasting until the mid-19th century. In 1868, Japan underwent the Meiji Restoration, which marked the end of its isolation and led to rapid modernization. This transformation allowed Japan to become a **powerful global player** by the early **20th century**.

Japan's involvement in **World War II** ended with its defeat and the devastating atomic bombings of **Hiroshima** and **Nagasaki**. After the war, the country underwent significant reconstruction, becoming a **pacifist nation** under U.S. occupation, while rebuilding its economy. By the 1960s and 70s, Japan had emerged as **one of the world's leading economies**, a position it maintains today. Combining a deep respect for its history and traditions with forward-looking technological and cultural innovations, Japan remains a major influence on the world stage. Today, Japan is associated with **cutting-edge technology**, including advancements in **robotics and electronics**, and is a **global leader in the automotive industry**. It is also known for its cultural exports like **anime**, **manga**, and **video games**, as well as its delicious cuisine such as **sushi** and **ramen**. Japan is admired for its rich traditions, including tea ceremonies and Zen gardens, while in its modern cities, fashion and a commitment to sustainability further define its global image.[2]

The Capital

Tokyo, the capital of Japan, is a bustling metropolis known for its **unique blend of modernity and tradition**. As one of the **most populous** cities in the world, it is a **global hub for business, culture, and innovation**. The city is home to towering skyscrapers, neon-lit streets, and cutting-edge technology, yet it also preserves its rich heritage through historic temples, traditional tea houses, and serene gardens. Areas like Shibuya and Shinjuku are famous for their **lively nightlife** and **shopping**, while places like Asakusa and Meiji Shrine offer glimpses of Tokyo's cultural and spiritual side.

---

2   https://asiasociety.org/education/japanese-history

Beyond its economic influence, Tokyo is a **center of art, fashion, and cuisine**, drawing visitors from around the world. The city's food scene is renowned, offering everything from Michelin-starred restaurants to casual street food. Tokyo is also famous for its **transport system**, known for being one of the **most efficient** and punctual in the world. With its vibrant districts, diverse cultural offerings, and cutting-edge developments, Tokyo remains one of the most dynamic and influential cities on the global stage.

The People

The people of Japan, known as **Japanese**, have a rich and complex history shaped by both indigenous traditions and external influences. The origins of the Japanese people trace back to the **Jomon period** (around 14,000 BCE), when the first settlers arrived from various regions, likely from mainland Asia. These early inhabitants developed unique tools, pottery, and hunter-gatherer practices. Later, during the **Yayoi period** (300 BCE – 300 CE), the Japanese population saw the introduction of rice farming, iron tools, and the influence of Chinese and Korean culture, particularly in language and writing. These early developments laid the groundwork for Japan's distinct identity.

Japan's history is deeply marked by its social structure, shaped around the concept of **community** and **social harmony**. Japanese people have historically placed great importance on **group cohesion** over individualism, which is reflected in everyday life, such as the practice of *wa* (harmony), where conflict is avoided, and cooperation is prioritized. The values of **politeness**, **respect**, and **humility** are fundamental in Japanese society, and these values permeate both personal interactions and business culture. For example, bowing is a common gesture of respect, and the language itself has various levels of politeness, depending on one's relationship to the other person.

Japanese people have a deep sense of **duty** and **responsibility**, influenced by centuries of feudalism and the prominence of the **samurai code of honor** (*Bushido*), which emphasized loyalty, respect, courage, and personal discipline. In modern Japan, these values continue to shape the workforce and education system, where hard work and dedication are highly respected. The idea of contributing to the well-being of society re-mains strong, as does the importance of maintaining a **balance** between the traditional and the modern.

Family is highly valued in Japan, and there is a strong sense of respect for **elders**, with multi-generational households still common in some areas. **Shinto** and **Buddhism** play significant roles in the spiritual lives of the people, guiding practices around life events like births, marriages, and funerals, as well as festivals that celebrate nature and the seasons. While Japan has evolved into a highly modern and urbanized society, traditional festivals like **New Year's Day, Obon**, and **Cherry Blossom Viewing** (*Hanami*) continue to hold great cultural significance, remind-ing people of the importance of nature, family, and seasonal change.

Despite Japan's reputation for collectivism, younger generations in-creasingly embrace individual expression, especially in areas like fash-ion, technology, and pop culture. Tokyo, for example, is a global hub for innovation, art, and entertainment, while still honoring traditional cultural practices like tea ceremonies and calligraphy. This balance be-tween honoring the past and embracing the future defines much of who the Japanese are as people.

Language

Japan's official language is **Japanese**, a language that has developed over centuries with influences from China, Korea, and other cultures. It uses **three distinct scripts**: Hiragana, Katakana, and Kanji. **Hiragana** is the basic script, primarily used for native Japanese words and grammatical elements, while **Katakana** is used for foreign words, names, and certain expressions. **Kanji** consists of Chinese characters that represent words or ideas, and a mastery of thousands of them is required for literacy. Japanese grammar is unique, often omitting the subject of a sentence, which is implied by context. The language also places a heavy emphasis on politeness, reflected in the use of honorifics, which convey respect depending on the social status or familiarity of the people involved in conversation.

Religion[3]

Japan is predominantly influenced by Shintoism and Buddhism, which have shaped the spiritual life of the people for centuries. **Shinto** is Japan's indigenous religion, centered around the belief in **kami**, spirits that are found in nature, objects, and ancestors. The practices of Shinto focus on purification, rituals, and celebrating the natural world, with many people participating in Shinto ceremonies at shrines, especially during life events like births, weddings, and seasonal festivals. **Buddhism**, introduced to Japan from China and Korea around the 6th century, has had a profound influence on the culture, particularly in matters of life, death, and spirituality. While Zen Buddhism, Pure Land Buddhism, and Nichiren Buddhism are some of the major schools, the practice of ancestor worship and death rituals remains central. Despite these two major religions, many Japanese people today identify as **non-religious** or **blended** Shinto and Buddhist practices in their daily lives, particularly during key life events or national holidays. Religion in Japan is not seen as something separate from life, but rather as a series of rituals and customs woven into the fabric of everyday existence.

Affordability

Japan can be both affordable and expensive for visitors, depending on the type of travel experience you seek and how you manage your budget. Generally, Japan is considered **more expensive compared to many other Asian countries**, especially in terms of accommodation, transportation, and dining in major cities like **Tokyo** and **Kyoto**. However, with careful planning and some smart choices, it is possible to visit Japan on a budget.

Accommodation in Japan ranges from budget hostels and capsule hotels to luxury resorts, so you can find **affordable options** if you look for guesthouses, capsule hotels, or even traditional ryokan inns that offer moderate prices for a cultural experience. Eating out can also be reasonably priced if you stick to conveyor belt sushi, ramen shops, or convenience store meals, which are both delicious and affordable.

---

3   https://www.japan-guide.com/e/e629.html

Convenience stores like 7-Eleven and Lawson offer a range of meals and snacks at reasonable prices, and many restaurants offer set menus or lunch specials that are budget-friendly.

Transportation, however, can be a **significant cost**. The Japan Rail Pass offers great value for long-distance travel between cities if purchased in advance, but local transport can add up, especially in Tokyo and other major cities where subways and trains charge by distance. Fortunately, Japan also has **discount passes for tourists** and extensive networks of buses and trains that make it relatively easy to get around efficiently without breaking the bank.

Japan, the Basics

How to Get There?

Japan is well-connected to the rest of the world, with several international airports serving major cities. The most common entry points for visitors are through four major airports, which handle a significant portion of international flights and are easily accessible from various destinations worldwide:

1. **Narita International Airport (NRT):** Located in Narita, about 60 km (37 miles) from central Tokyo, Narita is the main international airport for long-haul flights. It is a hub for international airlines and handles flights from all over the world.

2. **Haneda Airport (HND):** Located much closer to central Tokyo, Haneda has recently expanded its international terminal and now handles a significant number of international flights, especially those from Asia and Oceania.

3. **Kansai International Airport (KIX):** Serving the Osaka region, Kansai is Japan's second-largest international airport and connects visitors to the western part of the country, including Kyoto, Kobe, and Nara.

4. **Chubu Centrair International Airport (NGO):** Serving the Nagoya region, Centrair handles a mix of international flights, especially to and from Southeast Asia, as well as domestic flights across Japan.

Major international airlines flying in and out of Japan include **All Nippon Airways** (ANA), **Japan Airlines** (JAL), and **United Airlines**, which provide direct flights from many global destinations. Other prominent international carriers include **Emirates**, **Singapore Airlines**, **Delta Air Lines**, **American Airlines**, and **Air Canada**, all of which offer frequent connections to Japan from Europe, North America, and other parts of Asia. Airlines such as **Cathay Pacific**, **Qatar Airways**, and **Korean Air** also provide service to Japan, particularly from the Middle East and Southeast Asia. These airlines, along with various budget carriers like **Peach Aviation**, **Jetstar Japan**, and **Vanilla Air**, ensure that travelers have a wide range of options for flying to and from Japan.

The Cheapest Times to Fly to Japan

The cheapest times to fly are typically during Japan's low travel seasons:

* **Late autumn** (November) and **early winter** (December, before Christmas) offer lower prices. The weather is cool, but not too cold, and there are fewer tourists.

* **Late winter** (January to early February), after the New Year rush, also tends to have cheaper flight options, although it can be quite cold in Japan.

The most expensive times to visit Japan are during:

* **Golden Week (late April to early May):** A major holiday period in Japan, when many locals travel and accommodation prices soar.

* **Obon (mid-August):** A time when many Japanese people return to their hometowns for family gatherings.

* **New Year (late December to early January):** A time of high domestic travel and holidays, making flights and accommodation more expensive.

Booking flights well in advance, typically **three to six months prior** to your trip, can also help secure better prices, especially if you're traveling during peak seasons. Additionally, flying mid-week (Tuesday or Wednesday) is often cheaper than on weekends. Keep an eye out for airline sales and discounts to find the best deals.

When to Visit?

The best times to visit Japan depend on what you're looking for in terms of weather, crowd levels, and activities. **Spring (March to May)** is one of the most popular seasons, especially because of the cherry blossoms (*sakura*), which bloom in April. The weather is mild, and the country's landscapes are stunning as the flowers bloom, but this is also the peak tourist season, so expect larger crowds and higher prices. **Autumn (September to November)** is another excellent time to visit, as the weather is still pleasant, and the changing colors of the leaves create beautiful scenery, particularly in places like Kyoto and the Japanese Alps. The crowds are lighter than in spring, but it's still a busy time, especially in October.

Summer (June to August), although warm and humid, offers unique experiences like traditional festivals and fireworks displays, such as the famous Gion Matsuri in Kyoto and the Sumida River Fireworks in Tokyo. However, it's also the peak season for domestic travel, so popular spots can get crowded, and prices can rise. Summer is also the rainy season in June and early July, so expect occasional showers. **Winter (December to February)** is less crowded, with cold weather ideal for skiing in Hokkaido or the Japanese Alps. Winter is also great for enjoying hot springs (onsen) and experiencing seasonal traditions, like **New Year's celebrations**. While this is a quieter time for most tourists, it's a high season for domestic travel around the New Year holidays.

Well-known festivals include **Hanami** (cherry blossom viewing) in spring, **Obon** (a festival to honor ancestors) in August, and **Awa Odori** (traditional dance) in Tokushima. Cultural events like **Gion Matsuri** in Kyoto and the **Sapporo Snow Festival** in Hokkaido (in winter) are also major attractions. Additionally, **Tanabata** (Star Festival) in July and **Shichi-Go-San** (a celebration for children) in November offer insights into Japanese traditions. While peak season offers lively festivals and breathtaking natural beauty, off-peak times allow for a more relaxed experience with fewer crowds.

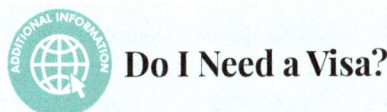 ## Do I Need a Visa?

Whether or not you need a visa to visit Japan depends on your nationality and the purpose of your visit. For many travelers, especially those from **visa-exempt countries**, Japan offers a **short-term stay** without requiring a visa.

Citizens of countries such as the **United States, Canada, European Union nations, Australia,** and several others can visit Japan for tourism or business purposes without a visa for stays of up to **90 days**. This typically covers trips related to tourism, business meetings, or short-term family visits. However, if you plan to work, study, or stay longer than 90 days, you will need to apply for a **long-term visa** before your trip.

Additionally, travelers who do not come from visa-exempt countries will need to apply for a **tourist visa** or another type of visa, depending on their purpose of visit. It's also important to check for any specific entry requirements, such as proof of onward travel or sufficient funds, as Japan has strict entry regulations, particularly related to health and safety measures. **Always verify the most current visa requirements with the Japanese embassy or consulate in your country before planning your trip, as rules can change.**

How to Get Around

Getting around Japan as a tourist is incredibly convenient due to the country's **highly efficient** and **well-connected transportation system**. The most popular and efficient way to travel between cities is by **train**, especially on the **Shinkansen** (bullet train). These high-speed trains are comfortable and fast, making them ideal for covering long distances between major cities like Tokyo, Osaka, Kyoto, and Hiroshima. For local travel, Japan's extensive network of **JR trains** and **subways** are very user-friendly and affordable. In major cities like Tokyo and Osaka, the subway systems are particularly convenient, offering quick access to popular attractions and neighborhoods. The stations are well-marked, and many have signs in English, making navigation easier for non-Japanese speakers. For visitors who plan to travel widely by train, the **Japan Rail Pass** is a great option, as it provides unlimited travel on most trains for a set period and is a cost-effective way to explore multiple cities. In addition to trains, **buses** are a useful option, particularly in more rural areas or places not easily accessed by rail. Many cities, like Kyoto, also offer special tourist buses that are designed to take visitors to key cultural sites. Although buses are a bit slower than trains, they offer a more scenic way to see the city.

Taxis are another convenient but more expensive option, especially when traveling short distances or to places that are less accessible by public transport. Japan's taxis are clean, safe, and operate on a meter, but they can become costly if used frequently. For those looking for a more leisurely way to explore, **bicycles** are an excellent choice, particularly in cities like Kyoto or in rural areas. Many places offer bike rental services or bike-sharing programs, making it an easy and eco-friendly way to get around.

Finally, for longer journeys, such as trips from Tokyo to Hokkaido or Okinawa, **domestic flights** are an efficient way to cover large distances. Japan's low-cost airlines, like **Peach Aviation** and **Jetstar Japan**, make flying affordable and accessible. Overall, Japan's transportation system is extremely well-organized and tourist-friendly, making it easy for visitors to explore both major cities and more remote regions without much hassle.

Monetary Advice

Japan's official currency is the **Japanese Yen** (**JPY**). The yen is abbreviated as ¥, and it's a decimal-based currency, meaning 1 yen is divided into 100 sen, though sen are rarely used in daily transactions. Banknotes come in denominations of 1,000, 5,000, and 10,000 yen, and coins are available in 1, 5, 10, 50, 100, and 500 yen.

The exchange rate between the yen and other currencies can fluctuate, so it's a good idea to check the current rates before your trip. As of the latest rates, **1 US dollar** (USD) is usually worth about **130–150 yen**, though this can vary. Currency exchange is widely available at banks, airports, and exchange booths in Japan, though the rates at airports may not be the best. You can also exchange money at your home country's currency exchange services before traveling to Japan. Keep in mind that exchange fees and commissions may apply.

Japan is increasingly **credit-card friendly**, especially in urban areas and major tourist spots. **Visa**, **MasterCard**, and **American Express** are widely accepted in hotels, department stores, and larger restaurants, as well as some convenience stores and vending machines. However, many smaller shops, restaurants, and rural locations may prefer **cash payments**. It's advisable to always carry some cash when visiting smaller establishments or more remote areas.

ATMs are also **widely available** in Japan, with most international debit and credit cards accepted at 7-Eleven ATMs, which are accessible in most cities. While Japanese banks often don't accept foreign cards, convenience store ATMs are an exception and a reliable way to withdraw yen. However, it's important to be aware of fees that might be charged for withdrawing from international accounts.

Foreign currencies like US dollars or euros are generally not accepted directly for purchases, so it's essential to have yen on hand. In some rare cases, larger tourist shops or hotels in major cities may accept US dollars, but this is not typical. Therefore, it's important to ensure you have the local currency or access to ATMs during your trip.

In Japan, **bargaining** is generally not part of the culture, and it is considered unnecessary or even **inappropriate** in most situations. Japan has a strong tradition of respect and honor, and transactions are typically straightforward, with prices being fixed. Whether you're shopping in a store, dining in a restaurant, or purchasing souvenirs, **the price you see is the price you pay**. Haggling over prices is uncommon and often unwelcome, especially in shops and markets, where fixed pricing reflects the cultural value of fairness and transparency. If you try to negotiate a price, it may cause discomfort for the seller since it goes against the norm of maintaining harmony and respect in business interactions.

Similarly, **tipping** is not a practice in Japan. In fact, offering a tip can be seen as **rude** or **confusing**, as service staff are already compensated appropriately for their work. Whether you're dining at a restaurant, taking a taxi, or staying in a hotel, there is no expectation of a tip. In some cases, leaving a tip may even be interpreted as implying that the service worker is not doing their job well enough, which is a sentiment that runs counter to the Japanese cultural emphasis on doing one's best and providing excellent service.

Instead of tipping, the Japanese show appreciation for good service in other ways, such as offering a **polite thank you** or simply expressing gratitude verbally. In restaurants, the service charge is typically included in the bill, so no additional tip is needed. Likewise, in hotels and taxis, you do not need to give a tip.

Japanese Hospitality

Japanese hospitality, known as "**omotenashi**," is rooted in a deep cultural respect for others, where hosts go out of their way to anticipate guests' needs and provide impeccable service. Japan is known for its **exceptional hospitality**, with a focus on **attentiveness, politeness**, and **creating a welcoming atmosphere**. *Omotenashi* involves not just fulfilling a guest's explicit requests but also anticipating their needs without them asking, ensuring a memorable experience.

Hospitality in Japan is often expressed through small gestures of kindness, such as offering tea, helping with luggage, or going out of the way to make guests feel comfortable. The attention to detail is remarkable, whether in a hotel, restaurant, or even when interacting with locals. In Japan, **politeness** is a cornerstone of daily interactions, and bowing is a common way to show respect. It's also customary to remove your shoes when entering someone's home or certain traditional accommodations like *ryokan*.

What is considered **polite** in Japan includes using **honorific language, bowing, offering gifts,** and **maintaining a humble demeanor.** Being **punctual** is highly valued since being late is seen as disrespectful. On the other hand, **impolite behaviors** include **raising your voice, speaking too casually** (especially with strangers or superiors), or **handling food or drinks in a careless manner**, such as sticking chopsticks upright into a bowl of rice, which resembles a funeral custom.

As a visitor, showing respect for Japanese culture involves adhering to their customs and being mindful of their space. It's important to bow as a sign of respect, be polite and humble, take off your shoes when entering certain spaces, and avoid making loud noises or gestures. Showing gratitude through simple phrases like *"arigatou gozaimasu"* (thank you) will go a long way in demonstrating respect for their culture.

CHAPTER 2
CUSTOMS

IN THIS CHAPTER

- Travelers Entering Japan
- Customs Entitlements and Monetary Restrictions
- Restricted and Prohibited Items
- Five Practical Tips to Know Before You Go

CHAPTER 2

CUSTOMS

Travelers Entering Japan[4]

When entering Japan, travelers must present certain documents and meet specific entry requirements. A **valid passport** with at least six months of validity beyond the intended stay is necessary. Depending on your nationality, you **may need a visa**, though many countries are exempt for short-term visits of up to 90 days. Additionally, you'll be required to complete an **Arrival Card**, which asks for details such as your intended length of stay and address in Japan. A **Customs Declaration Form** may also be needed, particularly if you're bringing items like large sums of money, food, or electronics.

Upon landing, the entry process in Japan involves passing through **immigration**, where you'll present your passport, visa (if applicable), and any required health documentation. Expect to have your fingerprints and photograph taken by immigration officers. After immigration, you'll proceed to **customs**, where you'll need to declare any items that need it, such as electronics or food products. Japan has strict regulations regarding what can be brought into the country, especially when it comes to food, plants, and animals. Once through customs, you'll **collect your luggage** from the baggage claim area, which is usually a quick and efficient process.

---

4   https://www.seattle.us.emb-japan.go.jp/itpr_en/
     TravelingJapanQuickFacts.html

Once you've completed all the entry procedures, you'll find several **transportation options** to get to your destination, including trains, buses, and shuttles that connect the airport to the city center. Japan's airports are well-organized, and the transport systems are user-friendly. As you interact with staff at the airport, remember that Japan places a strong emphasis on politeness and respect, so it's customary to bow and remain courteous in all public spaces. The process of entering Japan is generally smooth and efficient, but it's important to follow the local customs and regulations to ensure everything goes without a hitch.

 Even with Japan's reputation for safety and hospitality, it's always a good idea to check the latest travel advisories before your trip. The most reliable travel advisory site for Japan is the U.S. State Department's travel website, where you can find information about Japan including safety and security, entry requirements, and current travel advisories, accessible at **https://travel.state.gov/content/travel/en/ traveladvisories/traveladvisories/japan-travel-advisory. html**.

Customs Entitlements and Monetary Restrictions

When entering Japan, there are specific customs entitlements and monetary restrictions to keep in mind. Japan has strict regulations about the types and amounts of goods and currency that travelers can bring into the country. Here are general guidelines on what you can bring into Japan:

Currency:

Japan does not impose a restriction on the amount of foreign currency (including Japanese yen) that can be brought into the country. However, if you are carrying **1 million yen or more** (approximately US$6,639.27), or the equivalent in another foreign currency, you must declare it to customs upon arrival. This is part of Japan's anti-money laundering efforts. If you fail to declare amounts over this threshold, you could face penalties.

Permitted Items:

- **Personal Items:** Personal belongings such as clothes, toiletries, and electronics (such as phones, laptops, and cameras) are allowed as long as they are for personal use. There is no restriction on items like books, magazines, or items necessary for your personal comfort during the trip.

- **Duty-Free Goods:** Japan allows travelers to bring in duty-free goods within certain limits:

  - **Alcohol:** Up to 3 bottles (maximum 1 liter, or 33.8 ounces, per bottle).

  - **Tobacco:** Up to 400 cigarettes or 100 cigars.

  - **Perfume:** Reasonable amounts for personal use.

- **Gifts and Souvenirs:** You are allowed to bring in gifts or souvenirs, if they are for personal use and not for resale. However, it's important to remember that excessive amounts of gifts or souvenirs may raise suspicion, especially if they are items like electronics, clothing, or accessories intended for commercial resale.

- **Food:** Some food items are permitted for personal consumption. Common items such as snacks, candies, and packaged foods are generally allowed. However, fresh fruits, meats, dairy products, and food that could be considered a biosecurity risk (such as plant-based products) may require inspection or be prohibited. Always check the current list of restricted food items.

- **Medicines:** You can bring personal medications for your own use, but they must comply with Japan's regulations. Some over-the-counter medications that are legal in other countries may be restricted in Japan. It's advisable to carry a **doctor's note** if you are bringing prescription medication. In general, any prescription medication containing controlled substances like narcotics or certain stimulants are prohibited.

- **Electronics:** Personal electronics such as smartphones, cameras, laptops, and other similar devices are allowed. However, large quantities of electronics may be flagged as potential commercial goods, so it's best to limit the number of electronics you bring.

- **Cosmetics and Toiletries:** Small amounts of cosmetics and toiletries for personal use are permitted. However, items in large quantities (like bulk purchases of lotions, creams, or perfumes) may be questioned.

 ## Restricted and Prohibited Items[5]

Japan has strict regulations regarding prohibited and restricted items to safeguard its public health, environment, and security. It is essential to be aware of these restrictions to avoid penalties or delays at customs.

Restricted items in Japan include certain foods, especially **fresh fruits**, **meats**, **dairy**, and **plant-based products**, which could pose a risk to agriculture or ecosystems. **Medicines**, particularly those containing controlled substances, may require special documentation or be prohibited entirely, so it's essential to carry prescriptions for any necessary drugs. **Plants**, **seeds**, and **soil** are also restricted due to biosecurity concerns, while **animals and animal products**, such as certain types of leather or fur, may require permits or be outright banned. **Excessive quantities of alcohol and tobacco** (more than three bottles of alcohol and 400 cigarettes) can raise suspicions and may lead to fines or confiscation if they exceed personal use limits.

Prohibited items include:

- **Narcotics:** Illegal drugs, including marijuana, cocaine, and other controlled substances.

---

5   https://www.customs.go.jp/english/summary/prohibit.htm

- **Weapons and Explosives:** Firearms, ammunition, explosives, and items that could be used as weapons, such as certain knives or sharp objects.

- **Counterfeit Goods:** Fake brand-name items or pirated products.

- **Pornographic Materials:** Explicit materials, especially those that may violate Japan's laws regarding decency.

- **Items that Endanger Public Health:** Any substances or items that are harmful to human health, including certain pesticides or chemicals.

- **Tobacco Products for Minors:** Tobacco and related products cannot be brought in for minors.

- **Endangered Species and Products:** Items made from endangered species, including ivory, certain animal skins, and other wildlife products protected by international law.

Bringing prohibited or restricted items into Japan can lead to serious consequences, including the **confiscation** of the items, **fines**, or even criminal charges. In cases involving illegal drugs, weapons, or other highly restricted items, travelers may face **deportation** and a **ban on re-entry**, either temporary or permanent. Additionally, offenders could be **detained** for investigation, leading to delays or further legal action. Severe violations can result in **imprisonment**, particularly for drug-related offenses, as Japan enforces strict laws with zero tolerance for such items. To avoid these consequences, it is crucial to familiarize yourself with Japan's customs regulations and ensure that you comply with all restrictions before traveling.

 For a more detailed and complete list of restricted and prohibited items, you can visit Japan's official customs website at **https://www.customs.go.jp/english/summary/passenger.htm**.

Five Practical Tips to Know Before You Go

1. **Always carry cash** as Japan is still largely a cash-based society. While credit cards are accepted in many places, especially in big cities, smaller shops, rural areas, and even some restaurants may prefer cash. ATMs in convenience stores often have English options, so withdrawing cash should be easy once you're there.

2. **Learn a few basic Japanese phrases.** Even though many people in Japan understand English, making an effort to speak basic Japanese, like saying *"arigatou gozaimasu"* (thank you) or *"sumimasen"* (excuse me), can go a long way in building rapport and showing respect for the culture.

3. **Be mindful of quietness in public spaces**, particularly on public transport. Talking on the phone, speaking loudly, or making disruptive noise can be seen as inconsiderate. This is important not just on trains but also in restaurants and public areas. Keep your voice at a low level to show respect for others.

4. **Remove your shoes** when entering homes, temples, ryokan (traditional inns), or certain indoor spaces. This is a deeply ingrained cultural practice, and failing to do so could be seen as disrespectful. Be sure to wear clean socks, as you'll likely need to take off your shoes at these places.

5. **Respect the line culture**. Japan has a well-established system of queuing, whether for trains, elevators, or even at the convenience store. Always stand in line and wait your turn—cutting in line is considered extremely rude. This reflects the deep value of social harmony and order in Japanese society.

CRIME IN JAPAN

CHAPTER 3
CRIME IN JAPAN

Overview

Japan is generally considered one of the **safest countries in the world**, with very low crime rates compared to many other nations. The overall state of crime in Japan is remarkably low, and the country enjoys a reputation for being exceptionally safe for both residents and visitors. In fact, Japan reports a mere 0.2 intentional homicides per 100,000 people, a figure that is notably thirty times lower than that of the United States.[6] Violent crimes, such as homicides or assaults, are rare, and property crimes, like theft, are also comparatively uncommon. Visitors overwhelmingly feel safe walking through cities, even late at night, and incidents involving tourists are minimal.

The **contributing factors to Japan's low crime rate** can be attributed to several social, cultural, and systemic elements. One major factor is the **strong social cohesion** within Japanese society, where there is a deeply ingrained respect for authority, law, and order. Additionally, Japan's **strict laws and regulations**, combined with a highly efficient and well-funded police force, contribute to the country's low crime rate. The **education system** also emphasizes respect for others and social responsibility, which reduces antisocial behavior. Furthermore, the **low**

---

6   https://www.rstreet.org/commentary/
     the-hidden-trade-offs-of-japans-crime-free-society/

levels of poverty and **relatively equal wealth distribution** in Japan also reduce the likelihood of crimes driven by economic desperation.

Crime trend rates in Japan have been generally **decreasing** over the past few decades. While the country saw a rise in certain crimes during the 1980s and 1990s, especially related to economic factors such as the bubble economy, the overall trend since then has been a **steady decline.** **Violent crimes** have consistently remained low, while **property crimes** have also seen a decrease, particularly after the 2000s. More recently, the number of **youth-related crimes** has dropped, although Japan still faces some challenges with **cybercrime** and **fraud**, especially as technology evolves.

While Japan remains one of the safest places globally, there are still isolated cases of crime, but they are typically not as prevalent or as violent as in many other countries. The overall trend is a continued **decrease in crime,** with the Japanese government focusing on adapting to modern challenges like cyber threats.

Crime Hotspots in Japan

While Japan is widely known for its low crime rates and safe streets, certain districts in major cities are considered hotspots for crime and safety concerns. These areas, often known for their nightlife, entertainment, or historical significance, have attracted attention due to rising incidents of petty theft, harassment, and even organized crime. Although they remain popular destinations for both locals and tourists, visitors are often advised to exercise caution when exploring these regions, especially after dark.

Kabukicho in Tokyo is a notorious red-light district in Shinjuku, known for its vibrant nightlife, host clubs, and adult entertainment venues. It is associated with organized crime, contraband, and various petty crimes such as scams and harassment, especially at night. Visitors are advised to be cautious due to the risk of theft and other safety concerns. Tokyo's **Roppongi** is a popular area for nightlife, attracting both locals and an international crowd. However, it is known for crimes such as drink-spiking and robberies. The U.S. Embassy has issued warnings about the district, urging tourists to remain vigilant when visiting bars and clubs there.

Shinsekai in Osaka, once a thriving cultural and culinary hub, has experienced increasing incidents of petty theft and public intoxication. As urban decay has affected the area, these safety concerns have become more prevalent among both locals and tourists. Also, **Kamagasaki** in Osaka, known as Japan's largest slum and a historic laborers' district, faces higher crime rates compared to other areas. The district struggles with socioeconomic challenges, leading to incidents of public intoxication and petty crime. These issues contribute to its reputation as an unsafe area.

Susukino in Sapporo is the largest entertainment district in Hokkaido, renowned for its nightlife and eateries. While it offers a lively atmosphere, it also has its share of crime, including organized illicit activities, harassment, and petty theft, especially late at night.

In terms of **international comparisons**, Japan's crime rates are **significantly lower** than in countries like the United States. For instance, **violent crime rates** in Japan are much lower than in the U.S., where homicide, assault, and gun-related crimes are much more common. According to global crime statistics, Japan consistently ranks among the safest countries, with one of the lowest homicide rates in the world, far below countries like the U.S., Brazil, or even much of Europe. While **petty crimes** like theft or scams are a greater concern in some areas of Japan compared to violent crime, these are generally more common in entertainment or tourist-heavy districts. They are still far less frequent than in major metropolitan areas of the U.S. Additionally, **gun violence** is virtually **nonexistent** in Japan, and the country's strict gun control laws contribute to the overall safety.

Crime Statistics

Despite Japan's global reputation for safety and low crime rates, Japan is not entirely free from crime, and there are a few issues that have come to the forefront, particularly in major cities.

In the urban centers, **petty theft** and **pickpocketing** are among the most common crimes. Although these incidents are infrequent compared to other countries, they still occur in crowded places such as public transport or tourist-heavy districts. Unattended bags, mobile phones, and wallets are prime targets for opportunistic criminals. Additionally, tourists may sometimes fall prey to **scams**. These range from deceptive taxi drivers to inflated prices for goods or services, particularly in nightlife districts like Kabukicho and Roppongi. Visitors might find themselves caught up in these schemes, either through language barriers or a lack of familiarity with local customs.

Another concern, especially in popular nightlife zones, is **harassment** and **sexual assault**. While Japan's strict social order typically ensures respectful behavior, certain areas, such as the busy streets of Kabukicho or Roppongi, have a reputation for attracting unwanted attention, especially toward women. Instances of inappropriate groping or verbal harassment in packed spaces like public transport have also been reported, particularly during rush hours.

Then there are the more hidden but serious crimes, like those involving **organized crime**. The *yakuza*, Japan's notorious criminal syndicates, maintain a low but persistent presence in some parts of the country, involved in illegal gambling, human trafficking, and even drug smuggling. While these activities are more often confined to certain sectors, the influence of organized crime still casts a shadow over regions like Kabukicho, which is known for its adult entertainment.

Despite these issues, **Japan's law enforcement** is widely regarded as **effective** and **efficient**. The country's police force is well-trained, approachable, and backed by a culture that deeply values law and order. Police stations, called *"koban,"* are a common sight, and the Japanese public generally holds a **strong trust in the police**.[7] This has contributed to Japan's reputation for low crime rates and a high conviction rate, which is bolstered by meticulous police investigations and stringent legal proceedings. While corruption does exist in any system, it is minimal

---

7   https://www.cbsnews.com/news/
    walking-the-beat-in-japan-a-heaven-for-cops/

in Japan's law enforcement, and this commitment to justice helps keep crime levels relatively low. The legal system itself, with its severe penalties for criminals, further discourages criminal behavior, fostering an environment of safety.

For **tourists**, while the overall risk of encountering crime in Japan remains low, certain districts, especially those associated with nightlife and adult entertainment, pose higher risks. **Drink-spiking** incidents, particularly in areas like Roppongi, are a concerning example. In these situations, unsuspecting tourists may be drugged and then robbed or exploited. These crimes are not as widespread as in other parts of the world, but they do happen, particularly in places where alcohol consumption is high.

Ultimately, Japan remains one of the safest destinations for travelers. However, as in any major city, awareness of potential risks—whether it's scams, theft, or harassment—can help visitors navigate these hotspots more safely. By remaining vigilant, staying in well-lit areas, and trusting their instincts, tourists can largely avoid falling victim to the types of crime that occasionally make their way into Japan's otherwise peaceful streets.

 ## Quick Safety Tips

- **Stay Alert in Crowded Areas:** While Japan is generally safe, petty theft and pickpocketing can occur in busy places like train stations or tourist spots. Keep your valuables close and avoid leaving bags unattended.

- **Be Cautious in Nightlife Districts:** Areas like Kabukicho and Roppongi are known for their nightlife, but they can also be hotspots for scams, drink-spiking, and harassment. Stick to well-lit areas and be wary of overly persistent individuals or suspicious offers.

- **Use Trusted Transportation:** Be cautious when using taxis, especially in busy tourist districts. Opt for official, registered taxis or rideshare services to avoid being overcharged or scammed.

- **Avoid Flashing Valuables:** Keep your phone, camera, and expensive items discreet, especially in public places. This reduces the risk of attracting unwanted attention.

- **Know Emergency Numbers:** In case of an emergency, dial 110 for police and 119 for fire or medical assistance. It's useful to have these numbers on hand, even though serious incidents are rare.

- **Be Mindful of Alcohol:** In nightlife areas, be cautious about accepting drinks from strangers to avoid the risk of drink-spiking. Always watch your drink being prepared and never leave it unattended.

CRIMINAL LAW VIOLATIONS

CHAPTER 4

CRIMINAL LAW VIOLATIONS

Marijuana and Other Drugs in Japan

Japan has one of the **strictest drug policies** in the world, and marijuana is no exception. The country maintains a strong stance against drug use, with severe legal consequences for even small quantities of illegal substances. This approach is deeply rooted in Japan's cultural and historical views on drugs, and marijuana, in particular, has a complex relationship in the country.

Cannabis wasn't always viewed through a lens of criminality. Historically, marijuana was used for a variety of purposes, including as a source of fiber for textiles and ropes, and even in religious ceremonies. In ancient Japan, cannabis was also used in traditional medicine. However, the relationship began to shift in the early twentieth century when Japan introduced stricter laws around cannabis, influenced by Western nations, particularly the United States. Following the end of World War II, the U.S. occupation forces helped implement strict drug laws, and marijuana was officially banned in 1948 under the **Cannabis Control Law**. This was part of a larger effort to curb the influence of drugs in post-war Japan, and marijuana soon became associated with criminality and a negative image that persists today. Over the decades, the stigma surrounding cannabis grew, and its cultivation, use, and distribution became seen as highly dangerous and harmful to Japanese society.

Despite the country's tough stance on drugs, there has been a growing global conversation around **medical marijuana**, and Japan is no exception. Medical marijuana is still **illegal** in Japan, but there are **limited exceptions**. In 2018, Japan approved the use of **cannabinoid-based drugs** like Epidiolex for certain medical conditions, particularly for severe epilepsy. These drugs are derived from cannabis but are highly regulated, and the process to obtain them is extremely difficult. The Japanese government maintains a firm position that marijuana has no legitimate medical benefits beyond those very specific cases. Public opinion is still largely against the use of marijuana for medical purposes, and there is little advocacy for widespread medical legalization.

Recreational marijuana is **completely illegal** in Japan, and the laws surrounding its use and possession are strict. The possession, sale, or trafficking of marijuana can lead to severe legal consequences. Individuals found with even small amounts of cannabis face **heavy fines**, **long prison sentences**, and can be subject to **police interrogation** for long periods. The penalty for possessing marijuana can range from **up to five years in prison**, while **trafficking** can lead to **severe sentences** of up to **seven years** or more, depending on the circumstances.[8]

Given Japan's strict laws regarding marijuana, it is no surprise it also has a highly prohibitive stance toward **synthetic cannabinoids** and other **illicit drugs** such as **methamphetamine, cocaine, heroin, LSD**, and **designer drugs**. The country treats drug-related offenses with severe legal consequences, including long prison sentences, heavy fines, and a strong social stigma. Japanese law enforcement takes drug-related offenses very seriously. **Drug testing** is common, and authorities have the power to arrest individuals suspected of drug use based on behavior alone. Even travelers passing through Japan should be aware of the country's **zero-tolerance policy** regarding drugs, including marijuana.[9]

---

8   https://www.japantimes.co.jp/news/2024/12/12/japan/crime-legal/
     japan-cannabis-laws/

9   https://www.worldnomads.com/travel-safety/eastern-asia/japan/
     japan-drug-laws-the-zero-tolerance-approach

Penalties[10]

In Japan, **drug laws** are **extremely strict,** and the penalties for marijuana and other drugs are severe, regardless of the quantity involved. The Japanese legal system does not differentiate much between different types of illegal drugs, meaning the consequences for possession, use, and trafficking are harsh across the board.

Penalties for Marijuana:

- **Possession of Marijuana:**

  - **Up to five years in prison** and/or a fine of up to **¥1 million** (approximately US$7,000).
  - For smaller quantities, the sentence may be on the lower end, but even minor offenses can lead to long sentences.

- **Trafficking or Distribution of Marijuana:**

  - **Up to seven years in prison** or more, depending on the amount.
  - Large-scale distribution or trafficking can lead to life imprisonment.

- **Cultivation of Marijuana:**

  - **Up to seven years in prison** and significant fines.
  - This is taken very seriously and can lead to severe legal consequences.

---

10 https://www.kansaigaidai.ac.jp/asp/pre-arrival/orientation-program/bank/

Penalties for Other Illegal Drugs:

Methamphetamine (Crystal Meth), Cocaine, Heroin, and Other Narcotics:

- **Possession:**

  - **Up to five years in prison** and/or fines.

  - Possession of small amounts may result in a prison sentence, but larger amounts can result in **10+ years in prison.**

- **Trafficking or Distribution:**

  - **Up to life imprisonment** in cases of large-scale trafficking or smuggling.

  - **Severe fines** in addition to long prison sentences.

Designer Drugs/Synthetic Drugs (e.g., Synthetic cannabinoids, MDMA):

- **Up to five years in prison** for possession and distribution.
- **Longer sentences** for trafficking or manufacturing these drugs.

Foreign visitors caught with drugs in Japan face severe penalties under the country's strict drug laws. Possession can result in **up to five years in prison** and/or hefty fines, while trafficking or distribution can lead to **life imprisonment.** In addition to imprisonment, foreign offenders are typically **deported** after serving their sentence and may be subject to a **permanent ban** from re-entering Japan.

Prescription Medication

When traveling to Japan, it's essential to be mindful of the country's strict regulations surrounding **prescription** and **over-the-counter (OTC) medications.** While Japan allows travelers to bring prescription medications for personal use, there are certain conditions and limitations that must be followed to avoid potential legal issues. For example, medications containing **narcotics** or **psychotropic substances**—such as strong painkillers, sedatives, or ADHD medications like Adderall—are closely regulated. Even if these medications are prescribed in your home country, some may be completely **banned** or **heavily restricted** in Japan.

To bring these types of medications into the country, travelers must apply for an **import certificate** known as *Yakkan Shoumei*. This certificate is required for any prescription drugs that contain controlled substances like **codeine** or **stimulants**, and the application should be submitted **at least one month** before your departure. If you plan to bring a one-month supply of medication, you generally won't face any major issues, but anything beyond that may require additional documentation or permission from Japanese authorities.

In addition to prescription medications, travelers must also be cautious with common **over-the-counter drugs**. While many OTC medications, such as pain relievers or antihistamines, are permitted, certain ingredients found in products sold overseas can be restricted in Japan. For instance, drugs containing **pseudoephedrine** (often found in decongestants) or **codeine** (found in some cough syrups) are heavily controlled. Even a small amount of these substances can trigger legal consequences. **It's important to double-check that the OTC products you're carrying are in compliance with Japan's strict regulations.**

If you happen to bring medication that is **illegal** or **unapproved**, the consequences can be severe. At the very least, your medications may be **confiscated** by customs officers, but in more serious cases, travelers can face **fines**, **detention**, or even **imprisonment**. Failing to declare your medication when entering Japan can also lead to significant penalties, including questioning by authorities and potential deportation. To avoid complications, always ensure your medication is in its **original packaging** and accompanied by the **prescription or a doctor's note** that clearly states it is for personal use. **When in doubt, it's best to declare any medication to customs upon arrival.**

 For more detailed information, please visit the U.S. Department of State at **https://travel.state.gov/content/travel/en/international-travel/International-Travel-Country-Information-Pages/Japan.html.**

 # General Questions

1. *Is cannabis legal in Japan?* **No.** Cannabis is illegal in Japan. The country has very strict laws surrounding marijuana, and it is classified as a **controlled substance** under the **Cannabis Control Law.** Possession, cultivation, and trafficking of marijuana are all prohibited, and violators face severe penalties, including imprisonment and heavy fines. Japan has a zero-tolerance policy when it comes to cannabis, and the legal system imposes stringent punishments for any drug-related offenses.

2. *Can I legally purchase marijuana in Japan?* **No.** You cannot legally purchase marijuana in Japan. Marijuana is illegal for both residents and visitors, and there are no legal avenues to purchase it in the country. Any attempts to buy or sell cannabis are illegal and punishable by law. Foreign visitors are also subject to the same laws, with severe penalties for possessing or trying to acquire marijuana in Japan.

3. *Can I have marijuana on my person or in my hotel room in Japan?* **No.** You cannot have marijuana on your person or in a hotel room in Japan. **Possession is illegal** and can result in **up to five years in prison,** heavy fines, or both. Japan has a zero-tolerance policy, and foreign visitors face the same penalties as residents, including **deportation** and a **permanent entry ban.**

4. ***Are there any exceptions to the possession and consumption of cannabis in Japan?*** **No**. There are **no exceptions** to the possession or consumption of cannabis in Japan. It is strictly **illegal** for both residents and visitors, with **severe penalties** for violations, including imprisonment, fines, and deportation for foreigners. Japan has a **zero-tolerance policy** toward marijuana, and no legal allowances exist, even for medical use.

5. ***What are the penalties for possessing and consuming other types of illicit drugs in Japan?*** Possessing or consuming any illicit drugs in Japan, including **methamphetamine**, **cocaine**, **heroin**, and **synthetic drugs**, is punishable by severe penalties. **Possession** can lead to **up to five years in prison** and/or hefty fines, while **trafficking** or **distribution** can result in **life imprisonment** and significant fines. Even small amounts of these drugs can result in harsh legal consequences. Japan has a **zero-tolerance policy** for all illegal drugs, and offenders face both criminal punishment and significant social stigma.

 ## Law of the Land Hypothetical

HYPOTHETICAL: *Sarah, a 28-year-old tourist from the United States, travels to Japan for a two-week vacation. Before her trip, she was prescribed a painkiller containing codeine for a recent injury. Sarah brings a one-month supply of the medication in its original prescription bottle, with the doctor's note explaining that it is for personal use. Upon arrival at customs in Japan, Sarah is questioned by authorities and informed that her medication contains a controlled substance in Japan.*

Can Sarah legally bring the prescribed painkiller containing codeine into Japan, and what are the potential legal consequences if she doesn't have the proper documentation?

ANSWER: ***No.*** *Sarah cannot legally bring the painkiller containing codeine into Japan without the proper documentation. Codeine is* *classified as a controlled substance in Japan, and even prescription medication containing it is subject to strict regulations. To legally bring this medication into the country, Sarah would need to apply for a **Yakkan Shoumei** (**import certificate**) before her trip. Without this certification, Sarah risks severe legal consequences, including the confiscation of her medication, fines, and potentially up to five years in prison for possession of a controlled substance.*

Therefore, travelers must carefully research Japan's drug regulations and obtain any necessary permits before bringing prescription medications containing controlled substances like codeine into the country.

 ## Takeaways

- Japan has one of the world's strictest drug policies, with severe penalties for possession, trafficking, or use of illicit drugs, including marijuana, synthetic drugs, and narcotics.

- Possessing drugs can lead to up to five years in prison, and trafficking can result in life imprisonment. Foreign visitors caught with drugs may face deportation and a permanent ban.

- Some prescription medications, like codeine and ADHD drugs, are tightly regulated. Travelers must apply for an import certificate (*Yakkan Shoumei*).

- Japan enforces a strict zero-tolerance policy on drugs, with harsh penalties for even minor offenses, regardless of the offender's nationality.

- To bring prescription medications into Japan, travelers must carry proper documentation and ensure compliance with drug import regulations to avoid confiscation or legal consequences.

ALCOHOL-RELATED OFFENSES

ALCOHOL-RELATED OFFENSES

Alcohol-Related Offenses

Alcohol has been a part of Japanese culture for centuries, with its consumption deeply embedded in religious, social, and cultural traditions. Historically, alcohol was used in **Shinto rituals** and **Buddhist ceremonies,** where *sake* (rice wine) played an important role in purification and offerings. Over the centuries, alcohol became a symbol of **social bonding**, with drinking often seen as a means of building relationships and maintaining harmony in both personal and professional contexts.

During the Edo period (1603–1868), **sake** became widely consumed across different classes, and drinking establishments like **izakayas** (Japanese pubs) became popular places for social gatherings. Today, Japan has a well-established drinking culture, and alcohol is viewed as a social lubricant used to foster connection, relaxation, and sometimes even stress relief.

Alcohol plays a prominent role in **everyday life** in Japan. It is commonly consumed with meals, during business meetings, social outings, and festive events like New Year celebrations. Drinking is often seen as an important part of **workplace culture**, with after-work drinking sessions (called *nomikai*) being a common practice for employees to bond with colleagues and superiors. This practice is so ingrained in the culture that it's often expected, and refusal can sometimes be seen as rude or dismissive. Public drinking is also common, and alcohol can be found at

convenience stores, vending machines, and **grocery stores**. It's socially acceptable to drink in public places like parks or on trains, though excessive drunken behavior can still be frowned upon.

Japan is famous for several traditional alcoholic beverages, including:

- **Sake:** A wine made from fermented rice, which is often consumed during religious ceremonies, celebrations, or casual meals.

- **Shochu:** A distilled spirit, typically made from barley, sweet potatoes, or rice. It has a higher alcohol content than sake and is a common choice in southern Japan.

- **Umeshu:** A sweet plum wine made from ume fruit, typically enjoyed as an aperitif or dessert drink.

- **Beer:** Japan is known for producing high-quality lagers, with brands like Asahi, Kirin, and Sapporo being popular domestically and internationally. Beer is often consumed with meals and during social gatherings.

- **Whisky:** Japanese whisky has gained global recognition for its smooth flavor and craftsmanship, with brands like Yamazaki and Hibiki being highly regarded.

Alcohol Regulation[11]

Yes, alcohol is **legal** and **widely available** in Japan. The legal drinking age is 20, and individuals must be 20 years or older to purchase alcohol. You can buy alcohol in many places, including supermarkets, convenience stores, vending machines, and bars. The drinking age is strictly enforced, and young people attempting to purchase alcohol underage are typically asked for identification. There are no exceptions to the legal drinking age, and it is enforced uniformly across Japan.

However, while alcohol is legal, **alcohol-related offenses** can lead to serious consequences. For example, Japan has **strict drunk-driving laws**, with a low BAC limit of **0.03 percent**, which is significantly lower than

---

11   https://www.nomunication.jp/japans-drinking-laws/

in many other countries. Penalties for driving under the influence include fines, imprisonment, and long-term license suspensions. Even **pedestrians** with a BAC over 0.03 percent can be fined or arrested if their behavior is deemed unsafe or disruptive. Offenders can face fines of up to **¥500,000** (approximately US$3,700), imprisonment for up to **five years** for serious violations, and a **one to three-year license suspension**.

In addition, there are certain **restrictions on alcohol advertising** in Japan, particularly to protect minors and avoid promoting excessive drinking. Alcohol advertisements cannot **target minors**, and they are prohibited from promoting **irresponsible drinking** behaviors (e.g., excessive drinking, drunkenness). Alcohol advertisements on television are restricted in terms of **timing** and **content**, particularly during family-oriented programming. The focus of ads is typically on the quality of the beverage, rather than social aspects like partying or heavy drinking. While alcohol brands are involved in sponsoring sports events and music festivals, there are efforts to limit the exposure to younger audiences. Alcohol brands are also not allowed to sponsor content that might encourage excessive drinking or is directed at minors, ensuring that their advertisements maintain a socially responsible tone.

 **Things to Remember**

- **Drinking Age:** The legal drinking age is **20**.

- **ID:** You need a valid ID to purchase alcohol if you appear underage.

- **Public Consumption:** It is generally legal to drink alcohol in public places, but disruptive behavior can lead to penalties.

- **Public Drunkenness:** Public drunkenness can result in fines or detention if it leads to disruptions.

- **Drunk Driving:** The BAC limit is **0.03 percent**, with penalties including fines, up to five years in prison, and license suspension.

- **Purchase of Alcohol:** Alcohol can be purchased anytime, but only by those at least 20.

- **Alcohol Permits:** No special permits are needed for private events, but approval is required for large public gatherings.
- **Illegal Alcohol:** While not widespread, there are isolated concerns about counterfeit alcohol and illegal imports.

 **General Questions**

1. *How does Japan enforce its alcohol rules to prevent underage drinking and drunk driving?* Japan enforces its alcohol rules by requiring ID checks for alcohol purchases, strictly regulating alcohol sales to minors, and imposing severe penalties for drunk driving, including fines, imprisonment, and license suspension.

2. *Can I possess an open container in public?* **Yes.** In Japan, it is generally **legal** to possess and consume alcohol in public places, such as streets and parks, as long as it does not lead to disruptive behavior.

 **Law of the Land Hypothetical**

HYPOTHETICAL: *Sarah, a 19-year-old tourist from Canada, is visiting Tokyo and decides to buy alcohol at a convenience store. She presents her passport to prove her age but is still asked to leave the store. She wonders why she was denied even though she showed her ID. Can Sarah legally purchase alcohol in Japan with her passport as ID, even though she is 19?*

ANSWER: *No. Sarah cannot legally purchase alcohol in Japan because the legal drinking age is* **20 years old.** *Even though she showed her passport, she is underage and prohibited from purchasing alcohol, regardless of whether she is a tourist.*

 **Takeaways**

- In Japan, the legal drinking age is 20, and individuals must present valid ID to purchase alcohol if they appear underage.

- It is generally legal to drink alcohol in public places like streets and parks, but disruptive behavior due to intoxication can lead to penalties.

- Japan has a very low BAC limit of 0.03 percent. Penalties for drunk driving include fines (up to ¥500,000), imprisonment, and license suspension.

- Alcohol advertisements cannot target minors or encourage excessive drinking, and are regulated in terms of timing and content, especially during family programming.

- Violations such as underage drinking, public drunkenness, and drunk driving carry severe penalties in Japan, including fines, jail time, and possible deportation for tourists.

LAW OF THE LAND JAPAN

FIREARM & AMMUNITION OFFENSES

FIREARM & AMMUNITION OFFENSES

Current Firearm Status[12]

In Japan, firearm ownership is **extremely restricted,** governed by the **Firearms and Swords Control Law,** making it one of the **most gun-controlled countries** in the world. The process for acquiring a firearm in Japan involves multiple layers of screening. Applicants must be at least **20 years old,** pass a **background check,** including criminal history checks, and a mental health evaluation. Only those with a clear record and who demonstrate responsible behavior are eligible. Even a minor criminal conviction or history of mental illness can disqualify an individual from obtaining a firearm.

Individuals who wish to own a firearm must complete a **government-approved gun safety course,** which includes written tests and shooting practice. Applicants must demonstrate competence in using firearms safely, as well as in handling ammunition. After obtaining a firearm license, gun owners must undergo **psychological evaluations** every few years to ensure they remain fit to own and operate a weapon.

---

12 https://www.mofa.go.jp/policy/un/disarmament/weapon/report0306. html

Even those who successfully navigate the process can only own specific types of firearms. In Japan, only **shotguns** and **air rifles** are generally allowed for personal use. Firearms for hunting purposes are the most common form of legal possession. The ownership of **handguns** and **automatic weapons** is entirely **prohibited**, and individuals are not allowed to possess firearms for self-defense or personal protection. Furthermore, firearm owners must comply with strict storage regulations. Guns must be stored in a **locked safe** or a similar secure location. In addition, ammunition must be kept separately from the firearm to prevent misuse or theft.

Police are involved at every stage of the firearm ownership process. After an individual passes the background checks and safety courses, they must apply to the police, who will determine if they are eligible to own a firearm. The police also perform regular inspections of gun owners' storage and ensure compliance with all regulations.

Possessing an illegal firearm in Japan can lead to **severe penalties**, including **up to 10 years in prison**. Even possessing parts of a firearm, such as the barrel or firing pin, can result in criminal charges. **Japan's legal system takes gun violations very seriously, and penalties for breaking the firearm laws are among the strictest in the world.**

Legal Requirements for Purchasing, Carrying, and Using a Firearm

After meeting all the stringent legal requirements to obtain a firearm license in Japan discussed above, there are additional safeguards in place to ensure that firearms are used responsibly.

Once a firearm is legally owned, carrying it in public is strictly prohibited. The only exception is for those with a hunting license, who may transport firearms to designated hunting areas, but they must be unloaded and securely stored during transit. **Concealed or open carry for self-defense is not allowed in Japan.** If someone is found carrying a firearm without proper authorization, they face severe penalties, including imprisonment.

The laws surrounding the **use of firearms** are equally stringent. While self-defense is allowed in Japan, using a firearm in self-defense is not considered acceptable. Firearm owners are permitted to use their guns only for specific, lawful purposes such as hunting or sports shooting, and these activities are tightly regulated. The discharge of a firearm, even on private property, is **prohibited unless it is for legitimate purposes** such as hunting or target shooting at an approved range. Any use of a firearm that leads to injury, death, or public endangerment is met with severe legal consequences.

Using a firearm illegally, such as in a violent crime or an unauthorized location, can lead to **long prison sentences**, including **life imprisonment** in some extreme cases. Gun crimes are taken very seriously in Japan, and the punishment for illegal firearm use is severe.

Firearm Restrictions for Visitors

In Japan, the possession or use of firearms is heavily restricted, and these **laws apply to both citizens** and **non-citizens**, including visitors. **Foreign visitors are not allowed to possess firearms** while in Japan, regardless of their country of origin or the legality of firearms in their home country. Japan has a zero-tolerance policy when it comes to firearms, and bringing a firearm into the country—whether legally or illegally owned—is a serious offense.

Visitors who are caught with firearms or ammunition in Japan can face severe penalties, including imprisonment and heavy fines. **There are no exceptions or special permissions for tourists to carry firearms**, and even possessing a firearm for sporting purposes, such as hunting or shooting ranges, is strictly prohibited unless specific, extraordinary circumstances apply (which would require a detailed and complex approval process).

Penalties[13]

In Japan, strict gun laws are accompanied by **severe penalties** for gun-related violations. The country has one of the lowest gun crime rates globally, largely due to its rigid regulations. **Possessing firearms** or ammunition without authorization can result in **up to 10 years** in prison and fines of **up to 1 million yen** (roughly US$7,000). Even using or **discharging a firearm illegally**, such as in an act of violence, could lead to a prison sentence of **up to 15 years**, or life imprisonment if someone is injured or killed.

Gun smuggling is also heavily penalized, with sentences ranging from **five to 10 years in prison**. The penalties are particularly harsh if firearms are linked to **organized crime**, such as the yakuza, and can result in **life sentences**. Japan's gun laws are designed to keep firearms out of the hands of the general public, and there are a few legal exceptions, such as for law enforcement officers, certain security personnel, and individuals who undergo a rigorous licensing process. However, even licensed gun owners must adhere to strict regulations on the types of firearms they may possess, as well as how they are stored and transported. Japan's commitment to keeping firearms out of civilian hands has resulted in an **overwhelmingly low gun crime rate**. In fact, gun-related deaths are incredibly rare, with the number often in the single digits annually, a stark contrast to many other countries, including the U.S., where gun violence is more common.[14]

---

13   https://www.sentencingcouncil.org.uk/sentencing-and-the-council/about-sentencing-guidelines/about-published-guidelines/firearms-offences/)

14   https://www.cnn.com/2022/07/08/asia/japan-gun-laws-abe-shooting-intl-hnk/index.html

 ## General Questions

1. *Is it possible to bring a gun into Japan for personal protection when visiting?* **No.** It is not legal to bring a gun into Japan for personal protection, even if you are just visiting. Japan's gun laws are extremely strict, and firearms are generally prohibited for civilian use. The country does not allow visitors to carry weapons for self-defense, and any attempt to bring a gun into Japan would result in serious legal consequences, including arrest, imprisonment, and heavy fines. To ensure safety, visitors are expected to rely on local law enforcement for protection rather than carry firearms themselves.

2. *Can travelers bring ammunition into Japan for shooting sports or hunting?* **No.** Travelers cannot bring ammunition into Japan for shooting sports or hunting purposes without proper authorization. Even if you are a licensed shooter or hunter in your home country, you must obtain permission before bringing ammunition into Japan. Failure to comply with these regulations can result in serious consequences, including arrest, detention, and possible deportation. It is essential to ensure that all necessary permits are in place before attempting to bring any firearms or ammunition into the country.

 ## Law of the Land True Story[15]

The assassination of former Prime Minister Shinzo Abe in July 2022 was a shocking and extraordinary event for Japan, a country known for its strict gun control laws and remarkably low rates of gun-related

---

15 https://apnews.com/article/shinzo-abe-japan-government-homicide-assassinations-8267d689b9f63d5461bddf4f880dddc3

violence. Abe was shot by Tetsuya Yamagami, who used a homemade firearm while Abe was giving a campaign speech in Nara. This act of violence sent shockwaves through a nation where gun crime is extremely rare. Japan reported only nine gun-related deaths in 2018, compared to tens of thousands in other countries, like the U.S.

Yamagami was charged with murder and violating Japan's stringent gun control laws. His motive was reportedly linked to a personal grudge against Abe's connections to the Unification Church, a controversial religious group. In response to the assassination, Japan's government tightened security measures for political figures, and local police leadership resigned. The case highlighted the country's unique cultural approach to firearms, where even a single instance of gun violence has a profound impact on the public consciousness.

 ## Takeaways

- Japan enforces some of the toughest gun control in the world. The process to acquire a firearm involves background checks, mental health evaluations, a safety course, and police approval. Only shotguns and air rifles are allowed, with handguns and automatic weapons banned.

- Foreign visitors cannot possess firearms or ammunition in Japan, even for self-defense or sporting purposes. Attempting to bring them into the country can lead to severe penalties.

- Japan imposes harsh sentences for firearm violations. Possessing an illegal gun can result in up to 10 years in prison, while using one in a crime can lead to life imprisonment.

- Firearms in Japan are limited to specific uses like hunting or target shooting. Carrying a gun for self-defense or discharging it outside legal purposes leads to strict legal consequences.

PROSTITUTION

CHAPTER 7
PROSTITUTION

Overview

Prostitution in Japan is technically **illegal**, governed by the **Prostitution Prevention Law** enacted in 1956, which criminalizes the exchange of money for sexual intercourse. Despite this, the law has loopholes that allow other forms of sex work to flourish in a legal grey area. For example, businesses such as **escort agencies, hostess clubs,** and **soaplands**— where the act of sex is not always the explicit exchange—are not strictly prohibited. These businesses often operate under local regulations and zoning laws, but the lack of clear legal frameworks leaves much to interpretation. While prostitution itself remains outlawed, activities like compensated dating, where payment is made for time rather than sexual acts, are not criminalized as long as the exchange doesn't explicitly involve sex.

In cities like Tokyo's **Kabukicho** or Osaka's **Susen**, prostitution-related activities occur openly in **adult entertainment districts**. While these areas are known for their adult businesses, there are no official "red-light districts" where prostitution is explicitly sanctioned by the law. Instead, these areas serve as hubs for the adult entertainment industry, and although prostitution may occur, the authorities take a generally relaxed approach, unless there are issues related to human trafficking, underage sex work, or forced prostitution. The lack of specific, designated areas for prostitution creates legal ambiguity, as many of these businesses operate within the boundaries of the law, provided they don't openly engage in illegal prostitution.

Sex workers in Japan, however, face little legal protection, as the law does not regulate their conditions or mandate specific requirements for them. Those working in legal adult entertainment venues may be subject to internal company rules or contract stipulations, but these regulations are often inconsistent and lack legal oversight. This leaves many workers vulnerable to exploitation, especially in illegal or unregulated sectors of the industry.

Despite these challenges, the Japanese legal system focuses its efforts on cracking down on activities such as human trafficking and underage prostitution, prioritizing the protection of vulnerable individuals over the regulation of consensual adult sex work. The **penalties** for prostitution-related infractions are **severe**, especially for those involved in illegal activities. Clients caught engaging in prostitution face fines and potential jail time, while those running brothels or engaging in organized prostitution face harsher sentences, including lengthy prison terms. The most serious offenses, such as **human trafficking** or **exploitation of minors**, carry severe penalties, including **life imprisonment**. These stringent punishments reflect Japan's strong stance against coercion and exploitation in the sex trade.

Prostitution Practices

As of 2023, the number of businesses operating in the Japanese sex industry is approximately 33,270, highlighting its **significant presence** within society.[16] While prostitution is officially illegal, various legal loopholes allow a wide range of sexual services to operate, often under the guise of adult entertainment. Additionally, a study highlighted that around half of Japanese men aged 20-49 have reported purchasing

---

16   https://www.statista.com/statistics/1194705/
     japan-number-businesses-sex-industry/

sexual services at some point in their lives, reflecting the normalization of such services among the general population.[17]

The annual revenue generated from Japan's sex industry is estimated at US$40 billion, demonstrating its substantial impact on the economy, particularly in urban areas.[18] Furthermore, specific segments of the market, such as teenage prostitution, have been estimated to be worth up to ¥54.7 billion annually, suggesting a robust undercurrent of youth involvement in this sector.[19]

In Japan, the landscape of prostitution encompasses various forms, some of the most notable of which include:

- **Street Prostitution:** This form often takes place in designated areas such as Tokyo's Kabukichō, where women may solicit clients openly. Despite the illegality of street prostitution, the presence of women engaging in *tachimbo* (a type of street solicitation) is notable, highlighting the social acceptance and the risks these individuals face.

- **Brothels (Soaplands):** These establishments provide bathing and massaging services that often transition into sexual activities. Soaplands operate with a cleverly crafted legal distinction, as they provide services framed as bathing assistance, where acts that might be construed as sexual are legally justified as consensual encounters between "romantically involved" individuals.[20]

- **Escort Services:** The escort industry involves women who provide companionship and various non-sexual personal services, although some may offer sexual encounters upon the client's request. The average price for escort services usually ranges between ¥12,000 to ¥15,000 per hour, which is about US$100-130. Many escort services

17 https://pubmed.ncbi.nlm.nih.gov/38871450

18 https://medium.com/@ashe.vader/the-40-billion-shadow-inside-japans-enigmatic-sex-industry-94b688b58059

19 https://www.japansubculture.com/sexnomics-japans-billion-dollar-sex-industry-and-the-pink-zone

20 https://www.vice.com/en/article/how-japans-secretive-soapland-brothels-operate

thrive in major urban centers and are accessible online, though the legality of the services offered can be ambiguous depending on the specific terms and conditions agreed upon by the parties involved.[21]

- **Online Prostitution:** The digital era has introduced a new facet to prostitution, with services now promoted via websites and social media platforms. In 2023, around 1,400 online adult video services were recorded, highlighting the expansive nature of the online adult entertainment industry, which frequently overlaps with prostitution-related activities.[22]

Police Enforcement and Public Perception

Local authorities in Japan take a mixed approach to prostitution. On one hand, the government's stance is strict, especially concerning human trafficking and illegal prostitution involving minors. There are regular **police raids on illegal brothels**, and authorities tend to crack down hard on organized crime syndicates that control prostitution rings. In adult entertainment areas, the police often work with local businesses to ensure that laws are followed. However, Japan's strict laws are somewhat paradoxical. While authorities focus on reducing **coercion** and **trafficking**, they tolerate the existence of businesses that operate in a grey area, such as **soaplands** and **escort agencies**, as long as the services remain veiled in ambiguity regarding the exchange of sex.

Public attitudes toward prostitution are **largely negative**, especially in relation to street prostitution, which is seen as a social issue tied to poverty or exploitation. On the other hand, activities like compensated dating or certain forms of adult entertainment, which are seen as more "commercialized" or "regulated," are less stigmatized. While there is still a cultural taboo surrounding sex work in Japan, the tolerance for adult entertainment businesses is higher than for other forms of prostitution, given their historical and **economic** roles in the country.

---

21 https://www.pleasureinjapan.com/blog/escort-services-in-osaka#

22 https://www.statista.com/statistics/1195879/
    japan-number-adult-video-online-shopping-services

Sex Trafficking and Exploitation

Sex trafficking and exploitation remain **serious concerns** in Japan, though they are often overshadowed by the country's low-profile approach to prostitution and adult entertainment. While the legal framework is stringent regarding human trafficking, these crimes continue to persist due to various factors such as organized crime involvement, economic inequality, and the exploitation of vulnerable individuals.

Certain areas, particularly large cities like **Tokyo** and **Osaka**, are more vulnerable to sex trafficking. These urban centers host entertainment districts and adult entertainment venues where women, sometimes coerced or deceived, are forced into prostitution. Popular tourist spots, as well as areas with a significant migrant workforce, can also be hotspots for trafficking due to the higher number of people seeking employment in the adult entertainment sector.

The most **at-risk demographics** are **young women**, including minors and **foreign nationals**, particularly those from developing countries. In many cases, traffickers exploit vulnerable individuals with promises of legitimate work in Japan, only to subject them to sexual exploitation upon arrival. Additionally, women from **lower socio-economic backgrounds**, including those with limited support networks, are often targeted by traffickers.

The Japanese government has made efforts to combat sex trafficking through strengthened laws, including penalties for traffickers and international cooperation with other countries to address cross-border trafficking. While Japan has ratified **international anti-trafficking agreements** and implemented stricter regulations, enforcement remains a challenge due to the hidden nature of these crimes. Public awareness campaigns and non-government organizations continue to work on educating citizens about trafficking, but more action is needed to effectively curb the exploitation of vulnerable populations.

 ## Sex Tourism and Public Health[23]

Sex tourism is a presence in Japan, though it is not as openly advertised or discussed compared to other countries with more visible sex tourism industries. It primarily involves both foreign visitors and local clients seeking adult entertainment, often linked to certain red-light districts or adult entertainment zones. While the government does not officially condone sex tourism, certain districts, such as **Tokyo's Roppongi** and **Osaka's Tobita Shinchi**, are known to attract tourists seeking adult entertainment, including prostitution.

Sex tourism in Japan is typically organized through **word of mouth** or **discreet advertisements** on the internet. There are websites, escort services, and even agencies that cater to foreigners looking for sexual services, sometimes offering tours of adult entertainment districts. These businesses tend to operate in a legal grey area, similar to other forms of prostitution, as long as they avoid directly advertising sex and maintain ambiguity about the exchange of money for services.

The **public health concerns** associated with sex tourism in Japan are significant. The most prominent issue is the transmission of sexually transmitted infections (STIs), including HIV. With a steady flow of both locals and tourists engaging in high-risk sexual activities, there is an increased risk of STI spread. Despite Japan's relatively low rates of HIV compared to other countries, the prevalence of other STIs, such as syphilis and gonorrhea, has been on the rise. This is particularly concerning in unregulated or underground settings, where health precautions may be less rigorously followed.

To address these concerns, the Japanese government, through various health campaigns, encourages regular testing and the use of protection in the adult entertainment industry. However, due to the nature of sex tourism and the difficulty in regulating informal sectors, there is a

---

23 https://en.ara.cat/misc/sex-tourism-the-other-side-of-japan-s-coin_1_5301176.html

continual challenge to fully control these public health risks. Awareness efforts, as well as partnerships between health organizations and the adult industry, aim to reduce the spread of infections, but the issue persists due to the clandestine nature of sex tourism.

 ## Tips to Avoid Being Solicited

In Japan, while prostitution is technically illegal, there are certain areas where individuals may still face unwanted solicitations, especially in entertainment districts. If you're traveling or living in Japan and want to avoid being solicited, here are some practical tips:

- Avoid areas known for adult entertainment, such as Roppongi in Tokyo, Kabukicho in Shinjuku, and Tobita Shinchi in Osaka. These places are where solicitation is most common.

- Politely refuse if approached by street promoters offering free drinks or directing you to clubs. These individuals may lead you to establishments that engage in solicitation.

- If solicited directly, remain polite but firm with a simple "No, thank you" and walk away. Japanese culture values respect, and a clear refusal usually suffices.

- Stay cautious in unfamiliar areas, particularly late at night. Pay attention to your surroundings, as some people in these zones may approach you for solicitation.

- Choose reputable hotels with solid reviews and avoid love hotels or those that cater to adult entertainment, ensuring a more comfortable and safe experience.

- Whenever possible, explore nightlife areas with companions. Traveling in groups reduces the likelihood of being targeted for solicitation.

Law of the Land Hypothetical

HYPOTHETICAL: *Sarah, a tourist visiting Japan, is staying in a popular entertainment district in Tokyo. One evening, while walking back to her hotel, she is approached by a man who offers her an "escort service," promising a luxurious experience in exchange for money. He hands her a card with contact details for the service and suggests that she might be interested in "something more private" if she contacts them. Is it legal for Sarah, as a foreign tourist, to engage in an escort service in Japan, and what legal risks could she face?*

ANSWER: *In Japan, engaging in prostitution or soliciting sexual services is illegal under the Prostitution Prevention Law. Even if the escort service doesn't explicitly offer sex, it may still be linked to illegal prostitution. As a tourist, Sarah risks legal consequences such as detention, fines, or deportation if involved in such activities, especially if the service is connected to organized crime like the yakuza. To avoid legal trouble, she should steer clear of any suspicious services.*

Takeaways

- Prostitution is illegal in Japan, but businesses like escort agencies and soaplands operate in a grey area, avoiding direct exchanges of money for sex.

- Sex trafficking remains a significant issue, with young women and foreign nationals being the most vulnerable, despite strong legal efforts to combat it.

- Sex tourism exists in areas like Roppongi and Tobita Shinchi, contributing to public health concerns like the spread of STIs.

- Authorities focus on human trafficking and illegal prostitution but tolerate adult entertainment businesses operating in a grey area.

- Prostitution is stigmatized, particularly street prostitution, while more regulated forms, like compensated dating, face less societal judgment.

LGBTQ

CHAPTER 8

LGBTQ

Homophobia in Japan[24]

Japan's historical relationship with the LGBTQ+ community is complex and has evolved over time. In the pre-modern era, Japan had a more tolerant attitude toward same-sex relationships, especially during the Edo period (1603-1868), when male-male relationships were often depicted in literature, art, and the samurai class. The practice of **shudo**—a mentorship-based relationship between an older and younger man—was common among samurai and other groups. At the same time, women's same-sex relationships, while not as visible, were also recorded in historical texts.

However, the introduction of Western values and Christianity during the Meiji Restoration (1868-1912) brought with it stricter views on sexuality. The government enacted laws that criminalized sodomy, reflecting a shift toward more conservative sexual norms. This pattern continued well into the twentieth century, with Japan maintaining a largely heteronormative and conservative stance on sexuality.

In contemporary Japan, the LGBTQ+ community is **generally marginalized**, and there are significant challenges when it comes to legal recognition and social acceptance. **Same-sex marriage remains illegal,**

---

24 https://www.hurights.or.jp/archives/focus/section2/2008/06/japan-and-sexual-minorities.html

and there are no national laws protecting LGBTQ+ individuals from discrimination. However, there has been some progress in recent years. For example, major cities like Tokyo and Osaka have implemented **partnership certificates** for same-sex couples, offering some legal recognition, although these are not equivalent to marriage.

The general cultural attitude toward LGBTQ+ individuals remains quite **conservative**, particularly in **rural areas**. There is a deep-seated cultural emphasis on conformity and group harmony, which often leads to a reluctance to openly discuss or embrace non-heteronormative identities.

Japanese society traditionally values family structure and roles, where marriage and reproduction are seen as important social duties. LGBTQ+ individuals may struggle to fit into this framework, as same-sex couples cannot legally marry or adopt children. Additionally, the influence of Shinto and Buddhism, which focus on spiritual purity and social harmony, has shaped a culture that often prefers not to address or recognize sexual diversity.

In the workplace and public life, LGBTQ+ individuals may face **subtle forms of discrimination**, such as being passed over for promotions or excluded from social circles due to their sexual orientation. However, younger generations are generally more accepting of LGBTQ+ rights, and there is an increasing push for better representation in media, education, and law.

Religious factors also play a role, though Japan is less religiously driven than many other countries. Shinto, Japan's indigenous religion, does not have explicit teachings on LGBTQ+ issues, and Buddhism tends to focus on personal spiritual growth rather than social matters. However, Christian missionaries during the Meiji era contributed to introducing conservative sexual values. These influences linger in more religiously conservative pockets of Japanese society, shaping attitudes toward LGBTQ+ individuals.

LGBTQ Legislation[25]

Japan has made some progress in LGBTQ+ rights, but the legal landscape is still relatively underdeveloped. Some key developments include:

- **Same-sex marriage is illegal in Japan.** Despite calls for legalization and growing public support, there is currently no legal recognition of same-sex marriage or civil unions at the national level.

- **Partnership certificates:** While same-sex couples cannot marry, partnership certificates are offered in several major cities like Tokyo, Osaka, and Sapporo. These certificates provide some social and legal recognition, such as access to housing and hospital visitation rights, but they do not carry the same legal weight as marriage and do not grant the same rights, such as inheritance or tax benefits.

- **Anti-discrimination Laws:** There are no national laws that explicitly protect LGBTQ+ individuals from discrimination in employment, housing, or public services. However, some local governments have introduced anti-discrimination ordinances. For instance, Tokyo and other cities have laws that prohibit discrimination based on sexual orientation and gender identity, but these protections are not nationwide.

- **Transgender Rights:** Japan does have a legal framework for transgender individuals, although it is restrictive. In 2003, the country passed a law allowing individuals to change their gender on official documents. However, the law requires individuals to undergo gender-affirming surgery and be single (without children) to be eligible for the change. This requirement has drawn criticism for being overly invasive and limiting the autonomy of transgender people.

While some cities have implemented protections against discrimination, there are **no broad, national anti-discrimination laws** that explicitly protect LGBTQ+ individuals. This leaves many LGBTQ+ people vulnerable to **discrimination**, particularly in areas like employment, healthcare, and public accommodations. Transgender people also face

---

25 https://izanau.com/article/view/lgbt-japan

challenges, as their gender identity is not widely recognized in all contexts, especially in workplaces and educational settings.

LGBTQ+ rights vary significantly across different parts of Japan. **Urban areas** like Tokyo and Osaka are **more supportive** of LGBTQ+ rights, with vibrant LGBTQ+ communities, pride events, and a greater acceptance of diversity in the workplace and public spaces. Tokyo, for instance, hosts one of Asia's largest Pride parades every year. In these cities, LGBTQ+ individuals are more likely to find supportive spaces, including businesses and social networks, though they may still face challenges in their personal lives. **Rural areas**, on the other hand, tend to be **less supportive** of LGBTQ+ rights. Traditional values and close-knit communities in rural Japan can result in greater social pressure and less acceptance of LGBTQ+ individuals. In these areas, LGBTQ+ people may experience isolation, limited access to resources, and a lack of safe spaces for expression. Coming out in these regions can be particularly difficult, and many individuals may choose to hide their sexual orientation or gender identity.

LGBTQ Tourism and Safety Concerns

LGBTQ+ tourism in Japan is still **developing** but has seen growth in recent years, particularly in urban areas. Japan is known for its strong cultural history, fashion, food, and technology, but LGBTQ+ visitors often seek destinations that provide safe, inclusive spaces where they can feel welcome. Tokyo's **Shinjuku Ni-chome** district, which is home to a large LGBTQ+ community, offers numerous bars, clubs, and entertainment venues catering to LGBTQ+ individuals. Additionally, events like Tokyo's **Pride Parade** and Osaka's Pride celebrations have helped establish Japan as a growing destination for LGBTQ+ travelers. However, compared to countries with more established LGBTQ+ tourism industries, Japan's offerings are still relatively modest.

Public displays of affection (PDA) between LGBTQ+ visitors are generally **not widely accepted** in Japan, particularly outside major cities. While Japan is not as overtly conservative about public behavior as some countries, there remains a **cultural preference for discretion**. In public spaces, especially in smaller towns and rural areas, PDA between any couple—regardless of sexual orientation—can attract unwanted attention and be perceived as inappropriate. However, in **more LGBTQ+-friendly urban areas** like Tokyo's Shinjuku Ni-chome, there is a **greater tolerance for PDA**. It is relatively common to see LGBTQ+ individuals holding hands or engaging in light affection in LGBTQ+-friendly spaces, but outside of these areas, it is advisable to be cautious.

Safety Concerns for LGBTQ Visitors

While Japan is one of the **safest** countries in the world in terms of general crime, **LGBTQ+ travelers** should still be mindful of potential safety concerns, particularly in less tolerant areas. LGBTQ+ visitors in Japan should keep a few key considerations in mind for a safe and enjoyable experience. **Social sensitivity** is important, especially outside major cities. In more rural areas, subtle discrimination may occur, and public displays of affection can attract negative attention. **Accommodation discrimination** is rare, but in less progressive regions, researching LGBTQ+-friendly hotels in advance is wise.

Japan lacks comprehensive **legal protections** for LGBTQ+ individuals, so while overt hostility is rare, subtle discrimination in areas like healthcare or housing can happen. However, these issues are generally non-violent and more about exclusion or bias.

Despite these challenges, Japan is extremely **safe** for LGBTQ+ travelers. Violent crime is rare, and public transportation is reliable. That said, common sense should be used, especially when traveling alone or at night in unfamiliar areas.

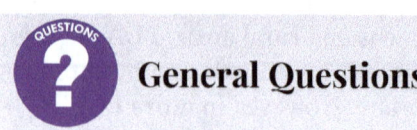

General Questions

1. ***Do laws in Japan protect homosexual expressions and conduct?*** Homosexuality itself is not criminalized in Japan, and same-sex relations between consenting adults are legal. However, Japan does not yet have comprehensive national laws specifically protecting LGBTQ+ individuals from discrimination. There are no nationwide laws recognizing same-sex marriage or civil unions, although some municipalities provide partnership certificates that offer limited rights.

2. ***What is the punishment for homosexual expressions and conduct?*** There is no punishment for homosexual expressions or conduct between consenting adults in Japan. Same-sex relations are legal, and there are no criminal penalties for such behavior. However, there are no legal protections against discrimination in many areas, such as employment, housing, and healthcare, which can create challenges for LGBTQ+ individuals.

Law of the Land True Story[26]

Taiga Ishikawa is a groundbreaking figure in Japan's LGBTQ+ movement, best known as the first openly gay politician to win a seat in Japan's Upper House. Coming out in 2002 through a memoir, Ishikawa became a vocal advocate for LGBTQ+ rights, founding Peer Friends in 2004 to support gay and male-identifying individuals. His election was a historic moment for Japanese politics, as he became the first openly gay candidate to seek leadership of a sitting parliamentary party. Ishikawa has been instrumental in advocating for same-sex

---

26 https://apnews.com/article/
uk-supreme-court-trans-gender-case-cf2bbc911c59b147a5261f431ee93eb7

marriage and LGBTQ+ recognition in Japan, using his political platform to push for greater societal acceptance and legal reform.

Despite the lack of comprehensive LGBTQ+ protections in Japan, Ishikawa's visibility and activism have made significant strides in the fight for equality. He has earned accolades for his work, including the Shivananda Khan Award at the APCOM's Asia Pacific HERO Awards. Ishikawa's perseverance in the face of societal and political backlash serves as an inspiration to LGBTQ+ individuals in Japan and across Asia, providing hope for a more inclusive future. His efforts reflect a broader regional movement toward recognizing and protecting LGBTQ+ rights, inspired by the progress made in countries like Taiwan.

Law of the Land Hypothetical

HYPOTHETICAL: *Hiroshi, a Japanese citizen, and his partner Kenji have been together for five years. They decide to move in together and want legal recognition for benefits like hospital visitation rights, inheritance, and tax benefits. They live in Tokyo, where LGBTQ+ partnership certificates are available, but they're unsure if these certificates will provide full legal recognition or be valid outside of the city. Additionally, they wonder if they're protected against discrimination in public or at work.*

ANSWER: *In Japan, same-sex couples can obtain partnership certificates in some cities like Tokyo, which provide limited benefits like hospital visitation rights. However, these certificates don't offer full legal recognition, such as inheritance or tax benefits, and aren't recognized outside progressive regions. Japan lacks national anti-discrimination laws for LGBTQ+ individuals, so Hiroshi and Kenji have no comprehensive legal protections against discrimination in employment or public services. They may face discrimination, with limited recourse, except through local ordinances or civil suits.*

CHAPTER 9

SEXUALLY MOTIVATED/ VIOLENT CRIMES

CHAPTER 9

SEXUALLY MOTIVATED/
VIOLENT CRIMES

Overview[27]

Sexually motivated crimes in Japan, including **sexual assault, harassment**, and **exploitation**, are a **notable concern.** While there are official statistics available, they likely underestimate the true scale of the issue due to the cultural factors that often discourage victims from reporting these crimes. The prevalence of these crimes is compounded by a combination of social, cultural, and economic factors that create an environment where sexual violence is sometimes minimized or overlooked.

The National Police Agency (NPA) reports **around 1,000 to 1,500 cases of rape annually**, including both completed and attempted rapes. **Indecent assault**, such as groping or unwanted sexual contact, is more common, with **5,000 to 7,000 cases** reported each year. However, these numbers are likely underestimates, as sexual harassment, particularly in public spaces like crowded trains, often goes unreported. There has been growing attention to **sexual exploitation** and **child sexual abuse**, including child pornography, and Japan has passed laws to increase penalties for such crimes. Despite these efforts, the prevalence of sexual exploitation remains a significant concern.

---

27 https://apjjf.org/2023/11/osawa

Sexually motivated crimes in Japan are influenced by several social and cultural factors. A significant barrier is the **social stigma** surrounding sexual violence, where victims often fear being blamed, especially if they were drinking or acting in ways deemed inappropriate. This discourages reporting and leaves many victims silent to avoid damaging their reputation. Additionally, Japan's **patriarchal society** and **ingrained gender roles** further contribute to the problem. Women's voices are often dismissed, and sexual harassment in both public spaces and workplaces is common, with few avenues for recourse. Cultural norms also prioritize group harmony over confronting uncomfortable issues, leading to a reluctance to address sexual violence openly. **Economic factors**, such as the dependence on men and the rise of precarious employment, make women more vulnerable to harassment and exploitation in workplaces, particularly where traditional gender roles are expected. These combined factors create an environment where sexually motivated crimes are **prevalent** but **underreported.**[28]

The most affected group in terms of sexually motivated crimes in Japan are **women.** Women are far more likely to experience sexual violence, harassment, and exploitation than men. In particular, **young women, workers in low-status or service jobs**, and those in **public transportation** or other public spaces are especially vulnerable to sexual harassment. According to surveys, around **40 percent of women** report experiencing some form of sexual harassment in the workplace, and **one in three women** report experiencing harassment in public spaces.

Another particularly vulnerable group in terms of sexual exploitation and abuse are **children.** Although child sexual abuse is difficult to measure due to underreporting, legal changes have made it easier to track such cases. **Sexual exploitation** in the form of **child pornography** has been an ongoing problem in Japan, though stricter laws have been enacted in recent years to address it.

While sexual violence is a nationwide issue in Japan, there are some regional differences in terms of how it manifests and is addressed. Large

---

28 https://english.kyodonews.net/news/2019/11/
e73ee06f884e-sex-crimes-remain-significantly-underreported-in-japan-govt-survey.html?phrase=environment&words=

urban areas like **Tokyo** and **Osaka** may experience **higher reported rates** of sexual harassment, particularly in public spaces like public transportation. In Tokyo, for instance, groping on crowded trains is a significant issue, leading to the implementation of women-only train cars during rush hour to reduce such incidents. However, **rural areas** or **smaller cities** may face challenges in dealing with sexual violence differently. Awareness and reporting may be even lower in these areas due to stronger social norms and closer-knit communities, where reputations are highly valued, and personal matters are kept private. Additionally, smaller communities may have fewer resources for supporting victims, leading to underreporting and less formal support for survivors. On the legal and policy side, larger urban centers tend to have more robust infrastructure for supporting victims of sexual violence, such as specialized police units and victim support centers, while rural areas may lack such resources.

Related Legislation

Japan has taken important steps in recent years to address sexually motivated crimes through legislative reforms and the introduction of various laws aimed at protecting victims and enforcing penalties for offenders. The country's legal framework on sexual violence is largely based on the **Penal Code**, which criminalizes rape, sexual assault, and indecent assault. **Rape**, as defined by the code, involves sexual intercourse without consent, and offenders can face prison sentences ranging from **three to 10 years**, with harsher penalties for aggravated cases. Similarly, **indecent assault**, which includes acts like groping, carries penalties of up to **10 years** in prison.

In 2017, Japan introduced significant **amendments to the Penal Code**, notably eliminating the requirement that victims physically resist an assault to prove lack of consent. This reform was a step toward recognizing modern understandings of sexual violence and making it easier to prosecute cases where victims may not have been able to resist. The revisions also introduced stronger sentences for severe sexual crimes, with some cases now subject to **life imprisonment**.

In addition to these changes, Japan's **Act on the Prevention of Child Abuse**, first passed in 2000 and amended several times, focuses on protecting children from sexual exploitation and abuse. The law criminalizes child pornography and sexual abuse, with offenders facing **imprisonment** and **fines**. Another significant piece of legislation, the **Anti-Sexual Harassment Law**, targets workplace harassment, requiring employers to take proactive steps to prevent harassment and ensuring that victims have recourse through legal channels. Businesses that fail to comply may face **fines** or even **civil lawsuits.**

The **Domestic Violence Prevention Law**, introduced in 2001 and revised in 2013, also plays a key role in protecting victims of sexual violence within domestic settings. The law allows victims to obtain restraining orders and provides police with the authority to temporarily remove abusive partners. Offenders can face prison sentences of up to **two years** or **substantial fines**. Similarly, the **Child Welfare Law** mandates the protection of children from sexual exploitation and abuse, allowing authorities to intervene and place victims in safe environments.

Despite these advances, **enforcement and implementation of these laws remain a challenge.** Many victims of sexual violence in Japan report a lack of support from law enforcement and difficulty obtaining justice due to cultural attitudes that still prevail in society and critics argue that the penalties for sexual violence are still too lenient in some cases, and further reforms are needed to ensure accountability. Moreover, Japan's legal framework for addressing sexual violence is also shaped by movements like **#MeToo**, which has highlighted the need for deeper societal and legal changes. Activists have called for more robust protections for victims, more severe penalties for offenders, and stronger enforcement of existing laws to ensure that those who commit sexual violence are properly held accountable.

General Questions

1. ***Do laws in Japan related to sex crimes protect the victims equally?*** **No.** Japan's laws against sex crimes have improved, but they do not always offer equal protection to all victims. While recent reforms, such as changes to the Penal Code in 2017, have made it easier to prosecute sexual offenses, cultural factors like gender inequality and victim-blaming still create barriers. Women, in particular, face challenges in reporting crimes due to societal stigma and a lack of trust in the legal system. Furthermore, marginalized groups, such as sex workers or minors, often do not receive equal protection. While progress has been made, disparities in enforcement and societal attitudes hinder full equality in victim protection.

2. ***Pursuant to law, what is the age of consent for sex in Japan?*** The **age of consent** in Japan is **13 years old** under the **Penal Code**. However, many local prefectures raise the age to **16 or 18** to better protect minors. Despite the low legal age, Japan has strict laws against sexual exploitation and statutory rape, with severe penalties for adults engaging in sexual activities with minors. The 13-year age of consent has drawn international criticism, leading to calls for raising the age to better align with global standards of protection for young people.

Law of the Land Hypothetical

HYPOTHETICAL: *Aya, a 22-year-old waitress in Tokyo, has been facing unwanted sexual advances from her manager. Despite feeling uncomfortable, she initially ignored the harassment out of fear of social stigma and potential damage to her reputation. After another incident,*

Aya decides to report the harassment to the police but is unsure if her complaint will be taken seriously due to her manager's position of power. Can Aya seek protection under Japan's anti-sexual harassment laws, and what are her legal options?

ANSWER: *Aya can seek protection under Japan's Anti-Sexual Harassment Law, which requires employers to prevent harassment and provide employees with reporting channels. If the employer does not act, Aya can file a complaint with the Labor Standards Office or take legal action against the employer for failing to comply. Aya can also pursue criminal charges under the Penal Code, which criminalizes sexual assault and indecent assault, with penalties up to 10 years in prison. Despite cultural barriers, Aya's legal options include filing a civil lawsuit against the manager or reporting the incident to the police. She can also seek support from victim assistance services to navigate the legal process.*

 **Takeaways**

- Sexually motivated crimes, including sexual assault and harassment, are significantly **underreported** in Japan due to cultural factors such as **social stigma**, **victim-blaming**, and a lack of trust in the legal system. This leads to an underestimation of the true scale of the issue.

- **Women**—especially young women, workers in low-status jobs, and those using public transportation—are the most affected by sexual violence, harassment, and exploitation. **Children** are also highly vulnerable to sexual abuse and exploitation, including in the form of **child pornography**.

- Japan's patriarchal culture and ingrained **gender roles** contribute to the prevalence of sexual violence, often minimizing or overlooking these issues. Victims, particularly women, are discouraged from reporting crimes due to fears of social consequences and lack of support.

- While Japan has introduced significant legal reforms, such as stronger penalties for sexual crimes and changes to the **Penal Code** (2017), these laws are not always effectively enforced. The penalties for sexual violence may still be considered too lenient, and further legal changes are needed.

- Urban areas like **Tokyo** and **Osaka** experience higher reported rates of sexual harassment, especially in public spaces like crowded trains. In contrast, rural areas have lower reporting rates due to stronger social norms and fewer resources for supporting victims.

ARRESTED IN JAPAN

ARRESTED IN JAPAN

Overview

When traveling in a foreign country, it's imperative to recognize that you are subject to the legal jurisdiction and regulations of that nation. These laws may significantly differ from those in your home country and might not offer the same legal protections you are accustomed to. It's crucial to bear in mind that penalties for violating foreign laws can be more severe than those for similar offenses in your home country, and ignorance of these laws is not typically accepted as a defense.

The consequences for breaking the law while abroad can be severe and may include expulsion, fines, arrest, or imprisonment. Even unintentional violations can lead to serious legal repercussions. It is essential for travelers to be aware of and adhere to the laws of the host country to avoid legal entanglements and ensure a safe and enjoyable experience. Specifically, stringent penalties are often enforced for possession, use, or trafficking of illegal drugs in many countries. Convicted offenders can expect severe consequences, including lengthy jail sentences and hefty fines. The legal processes for foreigners in the event of an arrest abroad involve being charged or indicted, prosecuted, potentially convicted and sentenced, and, if applicable, going through an appeals process.

Navigating a foreign legal system can be complex, and individuals arrested abroad must be prepared to comply with the legal procedures of the host country. Seeking legal representation and understanding the local legal nuances are crucial steps for those facing legal issues in a foreign jurisdiction. Awareness of and adherence to the laws of a foreign country are paramount when traveling. Understanding the potential consequences for legal violations and being prepared to navigate the legal system of the host country are essential aspects of responsible international travel.

Arrest Process[29]

In Japan, the **arrest process** begins when police detain a suspect, either with a **valid arrest warrant** or if the crime is committed in their presence. If the arrest is made **without a warrant**, the suspect can be held for up to **72 hours** without formal charges. During this period, police will conduct interrogations and gather evidence. If they need more time to investigate, they must seek approval from a **prosecutor** to extend the detention for an additional **10 days**.

During this detention period, the suspect undergoes **interrogation** by police, and this process is often long and intense. One key feature of the Japanese legal system is that **suspects are not guaranteed access to a lawyer during interrogation** unless charges are filed. This lack of legal counsel during questioning has raised concerns about the potential for **coerced confessions**. In many cases, suspects may confess to crimes, as confessions are a central part of the legal process, though these confessions may not always reflect the truth.

After the interrogation and extended detention, the **prosecutor** decides whether to file **formal charges**. If the prosecutor chooses not to charge, the suspect is released, but if they decide to press charges, the case moves forward. The prosecutor may choose to dismiss the case if the evidence is insufficient, or they may continue with prosecution.

Once formal charges are made, the case moves to **trial** in a **district court**. Japan's justice system is known for its **high conviction rates**, largely because cases with weak evidence are rarely brought to trial. Defendants

---

29 https://travel.gc.ca/travelling/advisories/japan/criminal-law-system

are entitled to legal representation, though the trial process is often swift, and there is little pre-trial discovery. As a result, the accused can face challenges in preparing an effective defense, especially when relying on the testimony of confessions.

Bail is **difficult to obtain** in Japan, particularly for serious crimes, and **pre-trial detention** can extend for weeks. Under Japanese law, persons suspected of a crime can be detained for 23 days without charge. The length of detention, up to the maximum period, is at the discretion of the public prosecutor and subject to the approval of local courts.[30] This extended period of detention before trial is one of the criticisms of the system, as many suspects remain in detention even before they are convicted. Only a small number of people can secure bail before their trial begins.

If found guilty, a defendant will face **sentencing** by the court, which may include **imprisonment, fines, or other penalties.** The Japanese legal system focuses on **rehabilitation**, and the country has one of the **lowest recidivism rates** in the world, but the process is often criticized for its reliance on **confessions** and the lack of robust legal safeguards for the accused.

In Japan, the **most common criminal charges** include **theft**, particularly shoplifting, which is prevalent due to the country's strict laws. **Drug offenses** are also frequent, with severe penalties for possession and trafficking, given Japan's tough drug laws. **Assault charges**, especially related to domestic violence or physical altercations, are common, as are sexual offenses such as rape and groping, which remain significant societal concerns. **Fraud**, including scams and financial crimes, is widespread, alongside traffic offenses, particularly drunk driving. While Japan experiences relatively few homicides, charges for murder or manslaughter do occur. Public disorder offenses, such as public indecency, and immigration violations, like overstaying visas, are also notable. Despite low

---

30 https://japan.embassy.gov.au/tkyo/arrests.html

overall crime rates, these offenses are actively addressed in the country's legal system. [31]

Rights of the Arrested Person

In Japan, arrested individuals are entitled to several legal rights designed to ensure fairness during the arrest and detention process. Upon arrest, individuals **must be informed of the charges** against them, though this may not always happen immediately. If they are detained without charges, they must be informed **within 72 hours.** One of the key rights is the **right to remain silent**; arrested persons are not obligated to answer questions or provide self-incriminating information, though police often strongly encourage cooperation, and confessions are crucial in many cases.

Arrestees also have the **right to legal counsel**, although access to a lawyer is limited, particularly during the early stages of detention and questioning. Lawyers are typically allowed to attend interrogations only after formal charges have been filed. For **foreign nationals**, there is an additional right to consular notification, meaning their **embassy** must be informed of their arrest, allowing the consulate to offer support and help arrange legal representation.

Within **48 hours** of arrest, the detained person **must be brought before a judge**, who will assess whether continued detention is justified. If the detention is extended beyond the initial 72 hours, the police must seek approval from a prosecutor for an additional 10-day extension. The individual also has the right to challenge their detention in court, ensuring that prolonged incarceration is subject to judicial review.

Japan's legal system prohibits **torture** and **inhumane treatment** during arrest and detention, although concerns about forced confessions persist. Additionally, while **bail** is difficult to secure in Japan, especially for serious charges, it is a right, and individuals can apply for release before

31   https://www.nippon.com/en/japan-data/h02253/#:~:text=Theft%20 accounted%20for%20nearly,since%202004.&text

trial. However, bail is often denied in cases where the prosecution fears the suspect may flee or tamper with evidence.

Foreigners arrested in Japan may face challenges such as **language barriers**, making it harder to understand legal procedures and communicate during interrogations. They also have the right to **consular notification**, meaning their embassy should be informed of their arrest, though this may not always happen promptly. Foreigners may struggle to access **legal representation** and experience **pre-trial detention** conditions similar to Japanese citizens. Additionally, **cultural differences** and the pressure to **cooperate** during questioning can complicate the process.

Getting Legal Assistance

Getting legal assistance in Japan can be a complex process, especially for foreigners, but there are systems in place to ensure that individuals are not left without help. When a person is arrested, they have the **right to legal representation, but access to a lawyer is often restricted during the initial stages of detention**. In practice, lawyers are generally permitted to meet with a detainee **only after charges are formally filed**, which can delay their involvement in the case.

For **foreign nationals**, navigating the legal system can be more challenging due to language barriers and unfamiliarity with local laws. However, foreigners arrested in Japan are entitled to **consular notification**, meaning their **embassy** or **consulate** must be informed of their arrest. The consulate can then provide a list of local lawyers, many of whom specialize in assisting foreigners and can help arrange legal representation.

 A list of local Japanese lawyers, provided by the U.S. State Department, can be accessed at **https://jp.usembassy. gov/services/attorneys/tokyo-lawyers/#tokyo.**

Embassies often serve as a vital bridge, offering support and ensuring that a foreigner's legal rights are respected. However, keep in mind, the consular powers are limited, and they cannot get U.S. citizens out of jail, provide legal advice or represent U.S. citizens in court, serve as official interpreters or translators, nor can they pay your legal, medical, or other fees.

In addition to private lawyers, Japan has a **legal aid system** to support individuals who cannot afford to hire a lawyer. This system, managed by the **Japan Legal Support Center**, provides **free or reduced-cost legal services** for people with limited financial means, as long as they meet the necessary criteria. This ensures that even those who cannot pay for private legal services still have access to professional legal assistance, particularly in criminal cases or civil matters.

For individuals who cannot afford a private lawyer, **public defenders** may be appointed once a case progresses to the indictment stage. However, public defenders often handle a high volume of cases, which may limit the attention they can provide. Despite this, they ensure that every arrested person has a lawyer to represent them in court.

Foreigners seeking legal advice can also reach out to law firms with international experience, as some lawyers in Japan specialize in cases involving foreigners. These firms may offer services in **English** or other languages, but such services can be more expensive. **Legal consultations** are typically available for an initial fee, allowing individuals to get basic advice about their legal situation. While legal fees in Japan can be expensive, especially for complex or foreign-language cases, the system does provide options. Lawyers may charge hourly rates or set flat fees, and individuals may need to pay a retainer before representation begins. For those who are financially eligible, legal aid offers a more affordable option.

Bail

Japan does have a bail system, but it is much more **restrictive compared to many other countries**. While bail is possible, it is not automatically granted, especially for serious crimes. After an individual is arrested and formally charged, they can be held in pre-trial detention for up to 23 days, and in some cases, this detention period can be extended. **The**

decision to grant bail lies largely with the prosecutor, who assesses the seriousness of the offense, the risk of the individual fleeing, and the possibility of interfering with the investigation. If bail is granted, the accused must pay a **bail bond**, which can range significantly depending on the severity of the charge and may **come with certain conditions**, such as restrictions on travel, regular check-ins with police, or limitations on communication with witnesses.

However, obtaining bail in Japan is often difficult. Prosecutors tend to oppose bail for serious charges, particularly in cases involving violent crime or high-profile offenses. **For foreign nationals, securing bail can be even more challenging**. Since foreigners are perceived as higher flight risks, especially if they lack strong ties to Japan like family or a job, bail amounts may be higher, and prosecutors may be more hesitant to grant it. Furthermore, language barriers and unfamiliarity with the legal process can complicate matters for foreign detainees.

If bail is denied, an individual may remain in detention for a prolonged period, sometimes months, while awaiting trial. The legal system in Japan places significant emphasis on pre-trial detention, and getting released before trial is difficult unless there is a strong case for bail. While foreign detainees are entitled to consular notification, meaning their embassy must be informed of the arrest, the embassy's role is limited to offering support and helping the individual find legal representation, rather than directly intervening in the bail process.

Complaints Against Police

In Japan, the police force is generally regarded as **highly professional**, with a strong reputation for maintaining public order and safety. Japan's police are often praised for their **efficiency, discipline, and low levels of violent crime**.[32] The **National Police Agency (NPA)** oversees law enforcement at the national level, while local police stations manage day-to-day operations in communities. The police are well-integrated into

---

32 https://www.cbsnews.com/news/
walking-the-beat-in-japan-a-heaven-for-cops/

the fabric of society, with police boxes (*koban*) found throughout neighborhoods, contributing to the public's sense of security.

Despite the generally positive perception, there are **complaints** and concerns about the police, which have occasionally sparked public debates. Common complaints against the police in Japan often relate to their **treatment of suspects**, particularly the practices surrounding **interrogation** and **detention**. The most notable issues include the extended periods of **pre-trial detention**, where suspects can be held for up to 23 days without formal charges, which critics argue can lead to **coercive interrogations**. Some reports claim that the pressure to confess during questioning can result in **false confessions**, particularly if the suspect is held in isolation for long periods without access to legal counsel.

Another common complaint is **racial profiling** or **discrimination against foreign nationals**. Foreigners, especially those who cannot speak Japanese fluently, may face difficulties during interactions with the police. They might be treated more harshly or be subjected to more scrutiny simply because of their nationality. **Police misconduct**, such as excessive force or mistreatment of detainees, is another area of concern. Although such incidents are relatively rare, they have occurred, particularly during arrests or protests. Concerns about the **transparency** of police actions have been raised, with accusations that the police are overly protected from accountability in cases of misconduct.

If someone wants to **file a complaint** against the police in Japan, there are several options available. Complaints can be directed to the **local police station** where the incident occurred, and there is a formal process for lodging grievances. The **Public Complaints Consultation Office** (which exists within local police stations) is the designated body for receiving complaints related to police conduct. Additionally, individuals can file complaints with the **National Public Safety Commission**, which oversees police conduct across the country. In cases of more serious misconduct, individuals can seek redress through the **ombudsman** system or file complaints with **legal aid services**.

It's important to note that **foreigners** can also file complaints, though they may face language barriers. Having a translator or lawyer may be necessary to navigate the process. Furthermore, if the complaint involves serious allegations, such as abuse of power or unlawful detention, victims may also seek legal assistance through the **Japan Legal Support Center** or contact their respective **embassy** for support.

 **General Questions**

1. *If I am convicted in Japan, am I likely to be released on bail pending the outcome of my appeal?* In Japan, being granted bail after a conviction, pending an appeal, is rare, especially for serious crimes. Courts are strict about bail requests post-conviction, focusing on the risk of flight or interfering with the legal process. The likelihood of appeals succeeding is also low, which further reduces the chances of being granted bail. Foreign nationals may face additional difficulties, as they are often seen as higher flight risks. Overall, while possible, bail after conviction in Japan is unlikely.

2. *What influences a bail determination?* In Japan, bail determination is influenced by factors like the **severity of the crime**, the **risk of flight**, and the potential for **tampering with evidence**. The individual's **ties to Japan**, such as family or employment, and their **criminal history** are also considered. For **foreign nationals**, the **perceived flight risk** is a major factor. Ultimately, the prosecutor and court assess these elements in deciding whether to grant bail.

3. *If I am arrested in Japan, how soon will I see a judge or magistrate?* In Japan, after an arrest, you will typically not see a judge or magistrate immediately. Instead, the police have up to **23 days** to detain you without formal charges, during which you will undergo interrogations. If the police wish to extend your detention, they must seek approval from a judge. You will only appear before a judge after this period if formal charges are filed, or if there is a request for your detention to be extended. The judge will assess whether to continue holding you during the investigation.

4. *How does the process of being granted bail in Japan differ for serious versus minor offenses?* In Japan, **serious offenses**, like violent crimes or drug trafficking, make it harder to obtain bail. Courts often view suspects as **flight risks** or potential threats to the investigation, leading to bail being denied or set at a high amount. For **minor offenses**, such as petty theft, bail is more likely to be granted, as the risk to public safety and the investigation is lower. **Ties to Japan**, like family or employment, play a significant role in securing bail for minor offenses. Overall, bail is more challenging for serious crimes and easier for minor offenses.

JAILS VS. PRISONS: CONDITIONS & CULTURE

JAILS VS. PRISONS: CONDITIONS & CULTURE

Overview

In Japan, the jail system is divided into two distinct categories: detention centers (often referred to as jails in other countries) and prisons. While both serve the function of detaining individuals, their roles, operations, and populations differ significantly. **Detention centers**, often likened to **jails** in other countries, are **short-term** facilities that house individuals awaiting trial or those serving short sentences. These centers are managed by local police departments, falling under regional police bureaus. When someone is arrested, they are typically taken to a detention center, where they will remain until their trial. Here, detainees may stay for a **few weeks** or **months**, but their stay is usually not prolonged. The primary purpose of these centers is to hold people temporarily while they await the legal proceedings, and the environment is focused more on maintaining security and order rather than offering rehabilitative programs. The detainees in these centers have not been convicted of their crimes, and the conditions are relatively minimal, with staff ensuring that individuals attend hearings and remain safe during their detention.

Once someone is **convicted of a crime** and **sentenced to a longer term**, they are transferred to **a prison**, which is managed by the Ministry of Justice. Prisons in Japan are for those serving longer sentences, typically more than a year, for crimes ranging from theft to more serious offenses. The main focus of prisons is not only to enforce punishment but also to facilitate **rehabilitation.** Life in prison is far more structured and strict than in detention centers, as inmates undergo a daily routine of work, education, and sometimes therapy. The aim is to prepare individuals for reintegration into society by providing them with vocational skills and educational opportunities. This rehabilitation-focused approach is central to Japan's criminal justice philosophy, which values the reintegration of offenders into the community.

Prison Conditions and Living Environment

In Japan, prisons are **highly structured environments** that prioritize **order, discipline,** and **rehabilitation.** One of the key aspects of Japan's prison system is the classification of inmates based on their security risks and the corresponding **security levels** assigned to different facilities. The prison system is divided into various **security levels**—from **minimum security** to **maximum security**—with the classification determining the type of housing unit an inmate will reside in.

Inmates who are classified as **low-risk** offenders, often those serving sentences for minor crimes or who exhibit good behavior, are housed in **minimum-security facilities.** These housing units are designed with a lower level of surveillance and fewer restrictions, and inmates here may have more opportunities for educational programs or vocational training. In contrast, those classified as **high-risk offenders**—typically individuals convicted of serious crimes or who have exhibited violent behavior—are placed in **maximum-security prisons.** These facilities are characterized by **high surveillance,** strict security measures, and more restrictive conditions. Inmates in these housing units may be isolated from other prisoners and subject to more frequent searches, limited movement, and tighter control over their daily activities.

Each prison in Japan is designed to match its level of security with its classification system, meaning that housing units are designed with **varying degrees of confinement.** Maximum-security units have more enclosed spaces, with high fences, guard towers, and constant monitoring. Medium-security units may have more relaxed rules in terms of movement and interaction but still maintain stringent security.

Minimum-security units provide inmates with more freedom, allowing them to move between different sections of the prison, work in workshops, or participate in outdoor activities as part of their rehabilitation.

While the security levels largely determine the daily living environment for inmates, the Japanese system also places an emphasis on **behavior-based classifications**. This means that inmates who demonstrate good behavior, cooperation with prison authorities, and progress in rehabilitation may be **reclassified** to lower-security units as part of their reintegration process. Conversely, inmates who engage in disruptive behavior or refuse to participate in rehabilitation programs may be **upgraded** to more secure facilities.

In addition to the classification of housing units, **access to healthcare** in Japanese prisons is an important aspect of prison life. All inmates are provided with **basic healthcare**, which includes access to medical services for general health issues, emergency care, and psychiatric support. Doctors, nurses, and psychiatrists are available to treat physical ailments and mental health issues, and each prison has its own medical facility for inmate care. Healthcare is generally well-organized, and inmates can request medical treatment through their prison counselors or directly from the medical staff.

However, **access to specialized care**—such as chronic illness treatment or advanced medical procedures—can sometimes present challenges. Prisons are not equipped to handle very complex medical conditions, so inmates who need specialized treatment are sometimes transferred to outside hospitals or larger medical facilities. For inmates with mental health issues, psychiatric care is available, but there are limitations in terms of resources and the availability of long-term counseling. The **mental healthcare system** in prisons, while present, can face challenges in addressing the underlying psychological issues that may contribute to criminal behavior. Japan's prison system has been criticized for a **lack of comprehensive mental healthcare**, particularly for inmates with severe psychiatric disorders.

Another important aspect of prison life in Japan is the provision of food, sanitation, and the fulfillment of basic needs. **Meals** are prepared in accordance with nutritional standards, and while they are simple, they are generally balanced and provide the necessary energy and nutrients for inmates. The typical prison meal consists of **rice, vegetables, fish,** and sometimes **meat** or **tofu,** reflecting the traditional Japanese diet. The meals are nutritious but plain, with little room for personal choice in terms of diet. However, the food is designed to maintain the health of prisoners rather than cater to taste or personal preferences.

Sanitation in Japanese prisons is a high priority. Prisons are known for being **clean and well-maintained,** with regular cleaning routines that all inmates must participate in. This emphasis on cleanliness is part of the broader cultural importance placed on order and respect for one's environment. Inmates are responsible for cleaning their own cells and communal areas, and failure to maintain cleanliness is seen as a violation of prison rules. The high standard of cleanliness not only contributes to the overall well-being of inmates but also reinforces the concept of **personal responsibility.**

In terms of **basic needs,** Japanese prisons are focused on providing for the **fundamental physical well-being** of inmates. Access to **clean water, proper clothing,** and **bedding** are basic rights that are strictly observed. Inmates are given uniforms, which they are required to wear at all times, and bedding that is simple but adequate for sleeping. While there is little in terms of personal comfort, the system ensures that inmates' basic needs are met to maintain their health and hygiene.

Inmate Rights and Legal Protections

In Japan, the rights and legal protections of inmates are shaped by a system that prioritizes **order, discipline,** and **rehabilitation.** While the Japanese prison system is often regarded for its efficiency and low recidivism rate, it is also known for its strict control over inmates. Despite these measures, prisoners still have certain **fundamental rights** and **legal protections,** though these may differ somewhat from those in other countries with more adversarial legal systems.

One of the key rights granted to inmates in Japan is the **right to legal representation**. Inmates are entitled to consult with a **lawyer** or **defense attorney**, particularly if they are involved in any legal proceedings, such as an appeal or parole hearing. This legal representation is crucial for ensuring that inmates can exercise their rights within the criminal justice system. Japan's legal system provides inmates with opportunities to challenge their convictions or sentences, although the process can be lengthy and difficult. Legal professionals can assist inmates in pursuing appeals or in seeking judicial review of their conditions.

Inmates in Japan also have the **right to communicate with the outside world**, albeit in a controlled manner. Letters are a primary form of communication, and while they are typically allowed, they may be monitored or censored for security reasons. The prison authorities may check letters to ensure they do not contain prohibited information, such as instructions for committing further crimes or messages that could disturb the order within the prison. Visits from family and friends are permitted, but they are usually limited and subject to strict regulations. Visits are monitored to prevent the introduction of contraband or unauthorized information, and inmates are typically allowed only limited physical contact with visitors.

Freedom of expression in Japanese prisons is restricted compared to what is generally expected in democratic societies. Inmates cannot freely express themselves through political speech, protests, or media engagement. This is in line with the overall emphasis on maintaining **discipline** and **order** in the prison environment. Inmates are expected to follow prison rules and regulations without engaging in activities that could disrupt the system. This includes **restrictions on media access**, meaning that prisoners have limited access to news or public information, and their communications with the outside world may be heavily monitored.

Regarding **healthcare**, inmates have the right to basic medical treatment. Every prison in Japan is equipped with **medical facilities**, where prisoners can receive care for general health issues, injuries, or illnesses. Inmates also have the right to seek **psychiatric care**, if necessary, although specialized mental healthcare can be more limited in some facilities. In cases where inmates require more specialized medical treatment—such as surgery or care for serious conditions—they may be transferred to external hospitals. However, the availability of mental health services, particularly long-term counseling, has been an area of concern in the Japanese prison system.

Labor rights for inmates in Japan are another aspect of legal protections, though these are framed within the context of **rehabilitation** and **restitution**. Inmates are required to work, and their labor is seen as part of their rehabilitation process. They may engage in various work assignments such as manufacturing, cleaning, or prison maintenance. While labor is mandatory, the work is structured to provide prisoners with skills that might help them reintegrate into society. However, unlike some systems in other countries, there is limited opportunity for inmates to earn **monetary compensation** for their labor.

Inmates also have the **right to be free from cruel or inhumane treatment**. Under Japanese law, as well as international human rights standards, prisoners are protected from torture, excessive punishment, or degrading treatment. While Japan's prison system is often criticized for its strict conditions, especially the psychological effects of long-term isolation or the rigid disciplinary methods, the system is designed to avoid physical abuse or torture. However, complaints regarding mental health, harsh solitary confinement, or excessive control over inmates' behavior do arise, with some human rights organizations calling for reforms in these areas.

The right to appeal is another significant legal protection. Inmates can appeal their convictions, sentences, or even decisions regarding parole. Japan has a court system that oversees these appeals, though the process is often seen as difficult and, in some cases, biased in favor of the prosecution. Parole hearings are held periodically to assess whether an inmate has shown adequate signs of rehabilitation to be released early. However, parole rates in Japan are relatively low compared to other countries, with many inmates serving the majority of their sentences before being released.

Finally, Japanese law provides for **religious freedom** within prisons, though the extent to which this is practiced varies. Inmates are allowed to practice their faith, and prison chaplains are sometimes available to assist with spiritual needs. However, religious practices are generally required to conform to prison rules, and in some cases, religious gatherings may be subject to restrictions in the interest of maintaining order.

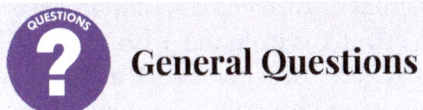

General Questions

1. *What is the difference between a jail and prison in Japan?* In Japan, **jails** (detention centers) are used for individuals awaiting trial or serving short-term sentences, usually under one year, while **prisons** house convicted offenders serving longer sentences and focus more on rehabilitation.

2. *Do jails and prisons offer religious services to inmates?*
   Yes. Both jails and prisons in Japan offer religious services. Inmates can practice their religion, with access to chaplains and services such as prayer or counseling, within the facility's rules.

3. *How do prisoners spend their time?* In Japan, prisoners spend their time following a highly structured routine. Their day typically includes work assignments, educational programs, and personal reflection. Inmates often engage in vocational training, participate in reading and writing courses, and attend psychological counseling. Free time is limited, and activities are designed to promote rehabilitation and self-discipline.

4. *What type of jobs can inmates perform?* Inmates in Japan can perform a variety of jobs, mostly centered around prison maintenance or manufacturing. These jobs can include tasks like cleaning, cooking, laundry, or working in prison-run factories, producing goods such as textiles, furniture, or electronics. The work is intended to help inmates develop practical skills for life after prison and contribute to their rehabilitation.

5. *How does the prison commissary system work in Japan?* In Japan, the prison commissary system is very limited compared to other countries. Inmates do not have the same level of access to a wide range of goods as they might in some Western prisons. Prisoners are provided with basic necessities like food, clothing, and hygiene items by the prison. Personal items such as snacks, extra toiletries, or small comforts are not available for purchase from a commissary. Instead, families or friends can send inmates a limited amount of money to buy items from the prison's approved store. This store typically sells basic items such as stationery or clothing rather than luxury or entertainment items. The system is very controlled, and everything inmates receive or buy is strictly monitored.

6. *What type of medical care do prisoners receive?* In Japan, prisoners receive basic medical care, including general treatment, injury care, and psychiatric support. Each prison has a medical facility with doctors and nurses, and inmates can be transferred to outside hospitals for specialized treatment. Mental healthcare is available but limited.

7. *What is prison culture in Japan?* Prison culture in Japan is characterized by a strong emphasis on discipline, order, and rehabilitation. Inmates are expected to follow a highly structured routine, maintain strict obedience to prison rules, and contribute to the upkeep of the prison through work programs. The culture values respect for authority, with little tolerance for disobedience or disruptions. Silence and routine are integral to daily life, and there is a focus on self-reflection and personal reform. Interaction between prisoners is typically limited to work or educational settings, as maintaining peace and order is prioritized. The overall goal of the prison system is to prepare inmates for successful reintegration into society.

HELPING A FRIEND OR RELATIVE IMPRISONED IN JAPAN

HELPING A FRIEND OR RELATIVE IMPRISONED IN JAPAN

Overview

If your family member or friend is imprisoned in Japan, the first step is to get in touch with the relevant authorities. It is important to locate where they are being held, so you can contact the local police station or the detention center directly. Once you know where they are, you can begin to address the situation more effectively.

A crucial next step is to **contact your home country's embassy or consulate** in Japan. The embassy can offer assistance by helping you understand the legal processes involved and may also help in locating your loved one if you do not have this information yet. The embassy is also a helpful resource for finding an **English-speaking attorney**. They can provide a list of lawyers who are familiar with the Japanese legal system, although they cannot represent you directly in legal matters. They can also assist with other practical matters, such as arranging communication with the detainee and facilitating consular visits to the detention facility, if possible. While consular visits are allowed, they may be subject to restrictions based on local regulations. If necessary, the embassy can help translate documents and communications if the detainee or their family does not speak Japanese.

Embassies play a critical role in providing **welfare services** as well. They can help inform you about your loved one's detention status, monitor their welfare during their stay in prison, and provide general legal guidance. While the embassy cannot intervene directly in legal matters or provide legal representation, they offer support by helping you understand the situation, directing you to legal resources, and ensuring that your loved one is treated fairly within the confines of the law. The embassy can also assist with **financial matters**, such as arranging for funds to be sent to the detainee if necessary.

It's important to remember that Japan's legal system operates differently from many Western systems, and the process can be slow. For example, individuals may be detained for **up to 23 days without charge**, a practice that is relatively common in Japan. In some cases, it can take months before a trial is scheduled. The conviction rate in Japan is very high, so it's crucial to understand the legal complexities from the outset. Keep in mind that all legal proceedings are in Japanese, so hiring a translator or using the embassy's services for translation might be necessary.

It is worth considering reaching out to support organizations that specialize in helping foreigners in Japanese detention, such as **prisoner advocacy groups**, most notably **Center for Prisoners' Rights (CPR)** and **Human Rights Watch**. These organizations may offer further guidance on navigating the system and provide support that can help you manage the emotional and practical aspects of the situation. While the process in Japan may seem daunting, contacting the right authorities and utilizing available resources can help ensure your loved one's rights are respected and that you receive the support you need.

Sending Food, Supplies, and Money to an Inmate

Sending food, supplies, and money to an inmate in Japan is subject to strict regulations. Japan's prison system has specific rules about what inmates can receive, and everything sent to them must follow these guidelines to ensure safety and maintain order.

In general, **food** cannot be sent directly to inmates. Japanese prisons provide all necessary meals, including basic food items like rice, fish, vegetables, and other staples. There are strict rules against sending food to ensure that nothing harmful or illicit is introduced into the prison. However, some prisons may allow for certain **care packages** containing **approved items** like toiletries, stationery, or clothing. These packages must be sent through the prison's authorized channels and meet the prison's specific guidelines. The items in these packages will usually be **monitored and inspected**. Inmates typically receive supplies directly from the prison system, but families can sometimes send a limited amount of personal goods like **toiletries** or **clothing**. It's important to check with the specific facility for what is allowed.

Money can be sent to inmates, but it must be done in a specific manner. **Prisoners in Japan are not allowed to hold cash directly**, so money is typically deposited into a designated **prison account**. Family members and friends can transfer funds through **bank transfers** or sometimes through **postal services**, depending on the rules of the specific facility. These funds can be used for purchasing approved items such as toiletries, clothing, and other personal necessities from the prison commissary. There are limitations on the amount of money that can be sent, and these rules can vary from one facility to another. Some facilities may allow family members to send money through the post, while others may require money to be deposited directly into the inmate's prison account.

It's important to contact the detention center or prison to confirm the exact procedures for sending money or supplies, as each facility can have slightly different rules regarding transfers. The embassy may also be a helpful resource in understanding these procedures, especially if you are sending money from outside Japan. In all cases, items sent to inmates must be carefully checked to comply with the regulations of the prison as any unauthorized goods will be confiscated. To avoid complications, it is best to work directly with the prison authorities or consult with a prisoner advocacy group for detailed instructions specific to the facility.

Mail, Phone Calls, and Visitation

Phone Calls

In Japan, the use of cell phones by inmates is strictly **prohibited.** Prisoners are not allowed to possess or use mobile phones during their incarceration, as this is seen as a potential security risk and a means of maintaining order within the facility. The authorities do not permit inmates to have access to unmonitored communication with the outside world via mobile devices.

However, inmates are allowed to **make and receive phone calls**, but this is heavily controlled. Phone calls are typically made through a **prison-operated phone system** that is monitored by prison authorities. Inmates can make **outgoing calls**, but these calls are often **limited in duration** and may only be made during specific times. The calls are generally made using a **pre-approved list of contacts**, and the prison authorities must approve the recipients of the calls. Incoming calls are not allowed, but prisoners can receive **letters**, and communication is usually carried out through this more-regulated channel.

Visiting

Visiting is allowed in Japanese prisons, but it comes with several strict rules and regulations. **Family and close friends** are typically allowed to visit, but visitors must be on an **approved list** provided by the inmate. It's essential to get the approval of the prison authorities in advance, as they need to confirm the relationship between the visitor and the inmate. **Spouses, children, parents**, and other **close family members** are usually eligible to visit, but **friends or extended family** may not always be allowed unless the inmate has specified them as an approved contact.

The frequency of visits varies depending on the specific prison facility, but generally, visits are allowed **once or twice a month**. The visits are usually supervised, meaning that inmates and visitors will not be alone during the meeting. Visitors are often required to follow a specific visiting schedule, and **appointments** must be made in advance. Visits are generally **brief**, and the amount of **physical contact** is usually **very limited** (e.g., no hugging or handshakes).

Before visiting, there are several important things to know. First, visitors will typically be required to go through a **security check**, where personal belongings will be inspected for contraband. **Food, drinks,** or **gifts** are usually **not allowed**, though in some cases, visitors may be allowed to bring **prescribed medicines** or **special items**, with prior approval. Visitors will be expected to follow the prison's rules regarding dress code, conduct, and behavior. A **polite and respectful attitude** is essential, as Japanese prison authorities maintain strict standards for **visitor behavior**.

Prison Scams

Prison scams involving inmates in Japan are **not** as **widespread** as in some other countries, but they do exist and typically target families or individuals unfamiliar with the Japanese legal and prison systems. These scams often prey on the vulnerability and stress of trying to support a loved one in prison. One common scam involves **individuals or groups pretending to be lawyers or legal experts**. They may promise to help get an inmate released or secure a favorable outcome in their case, often in exchange for large upfront fees for "legal services" or expenses that do not exist. Another prevalent scam is related to bail. Scammers may claim that an inmate can be released on bail, but only if a substantial sum of money is deposited quickly. These claims are often fabricated, as bail is rarely granted in Japan, especially for serious offenses, and is typically reserved for certain cases.

In some instances, criminals may **impersonate an inmate and contact their family**, claiming they need money for emergencies, such as medical treatment or special circumstances that require financial assistance. These phone calls are often made from prison phones, which might appear legitimate, making the scam even more convincing. Another type of scam targets families with **urgent requests for money**, claiming that an emergency situation requires immediate financial support. The scammer might suggest that the money is needed for medical treatment or some other pressing issue, pressuring the family to act quickly.

There are several **red flags** to look out for to avoid falling victim to these scams. One of the most important warning signs is being asked to send money through untraceable methods such as wire transfers, gift cards, or via third-party individuals. Legitimate institutions and authorities will not request money in these forms. Another red flag is a **sense of urgency**, where scammers pressure you into making quick decisions, often claiming that immediate action is required to prevent dire consequences, like a long prison sentence or urgent medical care. If someone offers a solution that seems too good to be true, such as promising a faster trial process or guaranteed bail for an inmate without proper legal grounds, it's likely a scam. Scammers may also avoid providing verifiable information, such as official credentials or contact details, so it's important to check any information you receive.

If you suspect you're being scammed, the first thing to do is to **stop all communication** with the individual or group immediately. Do not send any money or share any personal information. To verify the situation, contact the relevant Japanese prison or detention center directly. You can also reach out to your country's embassy or consulate for assistance in confirming the legitimacy of the situation. **Reporting the scam** to local authorities in Japan is also important, whether it's through the Japanese police or your embassy. If you received the scam communication by phone or email, make sure to report it to the appropriate authorities for investigation.

If legal assistance is needed, it's essential to work directly with certified lawyers. You can obtain a list of reputable attorneys from the embassy or through official legal associations such as the **Japan Federation of Bar Associations**. It's important to avoid using any contact provided by someone involved in the scam, as they are likely not trustworthy. Finally, educating others about these scams is crucial to help prevent others from falling victim to similar schemes. By staying alert, verifying information, and communicating only through official channels, you can protect yourself and your loved ones from these fraudulent tactics.

Upon Release

Upon release, foreigners in Japan may face several regulations and legal obligations depending on the circumstances of their case. One key consideration is **deportation**. Foreign nationals convicted of serious crimes, such as drug offenses or violent crimes, are often subject to deportation after serving their sentence. The Japanese government may revoke their visa or residency status, and they may be required to leave the country. If deportation is delayed, they may be detained while awaiting deportation procedures.

Additionally, foreign nationals may face a **ban on re-entry** to Japan, either temporarily or indefinitely, depending on the severity of the offense. Those who are allowed to stay in Japan after their release often have to comply with various legal obligations. This can include regular **reporting to immigration authorities** or **police**, and in some cases, being placed under **supervised probation**, which might restrict movement or require participation in rehabilitation programs. Violating these conditions can result in re-incarceration.

For those wishing to remain in Japan, foreigners must also provide **proof of financial support or legal residence**. Without proper documentation, they may struggle to find housing or employment, and their movement could be limited. Foreign nationals are advised to seek legal counsel to navigate these complexities, especially if they wish to stay in Japan or contest any aspects of their release or deportation.

THE ADMINISTRATION OF JUSTICE

THE ADMINISTRATION OF JUSTICE

Japan's Legal System[33]

Japan's legal system is a **civil law system**, heavily influenced by European legal traditions, particularly the German and French systems. It is based on written laws, and the primary source of law is the **Constitution of Japan**, which was adopted in 1947 after World War II. The legal system in Japan is characterized by a **strong emphasis on order**, **efficiency**, and **social harmony**.

Japan's legal system is **hierarchical**, meaning laws at the top, such as the Constitution, take precedence over other legal norms. Below the **Constitution**, there are **statutes**, which are laws passed by the National Diet (Japan's legislature). These include civil laws (e.g., the Civil Code), criminal laws (e.g., the Penal Code), and administrative laws, as well as regulations enacted by various government agencies.

The Japanese legal system operates with a combination of both **written** and **judicial law**. While judges apply written statutes to individual cases, they are also able to interpret and develop the law through case law, though judicial precedent is not as significant in Japan as in common law

---

33 https://www.nichibenren.or.jp/en/about/judicial_system/judicial_system.
html

systems like the United States or the UK. The judiciary is independent of the executive and legislative branches, but the courts are considered to play a more passive role in interpreting laws compared to systems in common law countries.

The courts in Japan are divided into several levels, with the **Supreme Court** of Japan being the highest. Below it are the **High Courts**, which are located in major cities and serve as appellate courts, as well as **District Courts**, which handle both civil and criminal cases at the first instance. There are also **Family Courts** and **Summary Courts** that handle less serious matters, including small civil disputes and minor criminal cases.

Japan has a unique system of criminal justice, which places a strong emphasis on efficiency and conviction rates. The prosecutors in Japan have significant power and discretion when deciding whether or not to prosecute an individual. In fact, **prosecutors control the case even before a trial begins, and Japan has one of the highest conviction rates in the world, often over 99 percent**. This high conviction rate is attributed in part to Japan's rigorous pre-trial processes, including the use of indictment without a grand jury system and extensive interrogations that can sometimes be controversial for their reliance on confessions.

The police in Japan are responsible for conducting investigations, and they can detain individuals for up to 23 days without charge, a period that is longer than in many Western countries. While there are protections against unlawful detention, critics have raised concerns about the treatment of suspects during this period, particularly regarding confessions obtained under duress.

In **civil matters**, Japan follows a **code-based system** where laws are written in **statutes**, and court decisions generally focus on interpreting and applying these codes. Civil disputes are often resolved through a **combination of mediation and litigation**, and there is a strong culture of settlement and compromise in the Japanese legal system.

Japan also has a **civilian jury system** for **criminal cases**, but it is limited. The **lay judge system**, which was introduced in 2009, allows citizens to serve as judges in serious criminal cases, alongside professional judges.

This system aims to make the legal process more transparent and ensure that it reflects public opinion, though it is not as widely used as in some other countries.

 **General Questions**

1. *Will the court treat first-time offenders and tourists with more leniency?* In Japan, the legal system is strict, but first-time offenders and tourists may receive some level of leniency, depending on the nature of the offense and the individual's circumstances. For first-time offenders, particularly in cases involving minor or non-violent crimes, the court may offer a more lenient sentence, such as a suspended sentence, fine, or probation, especially if the offender shows remorse and takes responsibility for their actions. The court may also consider the offender's lack of a criminal record and character when determining the penalty.

   For tourists, leniency is more situational. If a tourist commits a minor offense, such as petty theft or a low-level drug violation, they may face a fine, be required to leave Japan, or be deported. However, serious crimes—such as drug offenses or violent acts—typically lead to stricter penalties, with little room for leniency. Tourists may also face deportation and a ban on re-entry into Japan, even if it's their first offense.

2. *If I am charged with a crime, which court is likely to hear my case?* If you are charged with a crime in Japan, the type of court that will hear your case depends on the severity of the offense. For minor offenses, such as petty theft, minor drug violations, or traffic-related infractions, your case is likely to be heard by a Summary Court. Summary courts handle less serious criminal matters and typically deal with cases involving low-level offenses. In these courts, the proceedings are faster, and they can impose lighter sentences, such as fines, short jail terms, or probation. These courts do not involve juries, and the decisions are made by a single judge.

   For more serious offenses, such as violent crimes or larger-scale fraud, your case would be heard by a District Court. District Courts handle the majority of criminal cases in Japan, including those that are more complex or involve higher penalties. They have the authority to impose longer sentences, including imprisonment. These courts also hear appeals from Summary Courts and handle cases that require a more detailed investigation. However, if your case involves particularly serious charges, such as murder or large-scale drug trafficking, it may be heard by the High Court after an appeal, or the Supreme Court in very rare instances for final judgment, particularly if a legal precedent is being set or a significant issue of law is involved.

3. *What is the standard of proof in a criminal case in Japan?* In Japan, the standard of proof in a criminal case is "beyond a reasonable doubt," meaning the prosecution must present evidence strong enough to convince the court that there is no reasonable doubt about the defendant's guilt. However, Japan's legal system relies heavily on confessions, and many convictions are based on confessions obtained during police interrogations. The high conviction rate, often exceeding 99 percent, is partly due to the prevalence of confessions, sometimes under intense questioning. While the prosecution must present sufficient evidence to meet the standard of proof, there is less emphasis on witness testimony or physical evidence compared to some other legal systems. The court evaluates whether the total evidence supports a guilty verdict beyond a reasonable doubt.

 **Law of the Land True Story**[34]

Carlos Ghosn's case is a stark example of Japan's controversial legal practice known as **"hostage justice,"** where **suspects can be detained for prolonged periods without charge** and are **often pressured into confessing.** Arrested in November 2018 on allegations of financial misconduct, including underreporting his salary and shifting personal financial losses onto Nissan's books, Ghosn was placed in solitary confinement at the Tokyo Detention House. Despite his repeated denials of the charges, his requests for bail were consistently denied. The decision to keep him in detention is reflective of Japan's legal system, which relies heavily on pretrial detention as an investigative tool, with prosecutors often waiting for confessions to secure convictions. In Ghosn's case, he remained in custody for over two months before his trial even began, a typical scenario for high-profile cases in Japan. This prolonged detention without charge and the high conviction rate, often achieved through confessions obtained under intense interrogation, have led to growing international criticism of Japan's criminal justice system.

 **Takeaways**

- Japan's legal system follows a civil law tradition, heavily influenced by Germany and France, with written laws, especially the Constitution, serving as the highest authority.

- Prosecutors have significant control over criminal cases, contributing to Japan's high conviction rates, which are often based on confessions obtained through extensive interrogations.

---

34 https://www.aljazeera.com/economy/2019/1/29/
    hostage-justice-how-japan-secures-confessions-and-convictions

- Suspects can be detained for up to 23 days without charge, a practice called "hostage justice," which is used to pressure suspects into confessing.

- Japan's courts include Summary Courts for minor offenses and District Courts for more serious crimes, with the possibility of appeals to High or Supreme Courts in significant cases.

- First-time offenders and tourists may receive more lenient penalties, such as fines or probation, for minor crimes. However, bail is rarely granted without a confession.

- The standard of proof in a criminal case in Japan is "beyond a reasonable doubt."

CRIME VICTIM ASSISTANCE

CRIME VICTIM ASSISTANCE

Overview

In Japan, crime victim assistance is provided through **a combination of government programs, nonprofit organizations, and support services** aimed at helping victims recover and navigate the legal system. Japan has a strong emphasis on societal harmony and the protection of individual rights, which extends to offering support to those who have suffered from crime.

Victim support services in Japan typically include emotional, psychological, and legal aid. Public organizations, such as the **Victim Support Center** and **National Victim Assistance Center**, provide resources for victims of various crimes, including domestic violence, sexual assault, and robbery. These centers offer counseling, information on legal rights, and help in navigating the criminal justice process. They also assist in connecting victims with medical care, financial compensation, and housing support, where necessary.

For victims of violent crime, Japan has a **Crime Victim Compensation Law,** which provides financial assistance for those who suffer physical or mental injuries due to criminal acts. This law offers compensation to victims who are unable to receive restitution through the criminal justice system, ensuring they have access to necessary resources for recovery. Japan has a dedicated **domestic violence hotline** and services dedicated to supporting victims of abuse, offering confidential advice and helping them find shelter and safety. These services have gained prominence in recent years, as awareness around issues like domestic violence and sexual assault has increased.

Another key aspect of victim support is **legal aid**. Victims can receive help from lawyers specializing in criminal law and victim rights, and there are also public legal consultation services available. The legal process can be complex, and many victims rely on these services to understand their options and ensure they are treated fairly in court.

What to Do If You Are the Victim of a Crime

If you are the victim of a crime in Japan, the first thing you should do is **ensure your safety**. If you are in immediate danger, it's crucial to remove yourself from the situation and **call the police at 110**. Once you're in a safe location, contacting the police to report the crime should be your next step. Be prepared to provide detailed information about the incident, including what happened, when and where it occurred, and any details about the perpetrator. The police may also ask for a statement, and you can request a police report, which will be important for any further legal or insurance processes.

If you've sustained any injuries, it's essential to **seek medical attention** right away. Even if you feel fine, it's advisable to have a healthcare professional examine you, especially in cases of assault or other violent crimes, as some injuries may not be immediately apparent. While waiting for the authorities to respond, if it's safe to do so, try to **gather any evidence** related to the crime. This might include photographs of injuries or damage, written records of threats or communications, or any other physical evidence that may be helpful. You should also **keep a detailed record** of what happened and any interactions related to the incident.

After contacting the police, you should **consider reaching out to victim support organizations**. In Japan, there are various centers and hotlines dedicated to assisting victims of crime. These organizations can provide emotional support, guide you through the legal process, and inform you about the rights you have as a victim. They can also help connect you with professionals who can assist with legal and medical needs. If you want to **pursue legal action**, consulting with a lawyer who specializes in criminal law or victim advocacy is highly recommended. A lawyer can help you understand your options, whether that involves filing a criminal complaint or pursuing compensation through civil courts. In Japan, the Crime Victim Compensation Law may also provide financial assistance to victims of certain crimes, so it's important to inquire about eligibility for these programs.

Throughout the process, **staying in touch with the police and any legal representatives is key**. This ensures that you are up to date on any progress in the investigation or legal proceedings. Additionally, don't neglect your mental health. Being the victim of a crime can be traumatic and seeking counseling or support from mental health professionals can aid in your recovery.

Common Tourist Scams in Japan

While Japan is generally considered one of the safest countries for travelers, tourists may still encounter certain scams. These scams, while rare, can be unsettling for unsuspecting visitors. One of the most common scams involves **overcharging or scams in taxis**. Although taxis in Japan have a regulated fare system, there are occasional reports of drivers taking longer routes or charging higher fares, particularly from airports or busy tourist areas. This is not typical, but it can happen, so always ensure the meter is running and agree on the fare beforehand if possible. Additionally, some taxis might not be fully honest about availability or try to take advantage of tourists unfamiliar with the area.

Another scam that tourists may encounter is **fake rental shops or services**. These might appear as legitimate businesses, offering items like high-end electronics or Japanese cultural experiences at "discounted" rates. Once tourists pay for these services or products, they often find the goods are of poor quality or never arrive. To avoid this, it's best to research rental companies online and check reviews before renting anything.

Street performers and beggars are another issue, though these scams are less aggressive in Japan than in many other countries. In certain crowded tourist areas, particularly in and around major temples or stations, you might find individuals asking for donations or using emotional appeals. While it's not inherently a scam, it's worth being cautious of individuals who might use misleading tactics to solicit money from tourists.

Charity scams are also a possibility. Some tourists have reported being approached by people claiming to represent non-profit organizations or causes. These individuals may seem very convincing but could be fraudulent. To avoid falling for such scams, it's recommended to avoid donating directly to street solicitors and instead support known charities through their official channels.

Lastly, **fraudulent ticket sales** can also be an issue, particularly with events, concerts, or theme parks. Some scammers sell tickets that are either fake or invalid. Tourists should always buy tickets from reputable vendors, such as official websites, authorized kiosks, or licensed agencies.

Although these scams are relatively rare, **staying vigilant, asking locals for advice when uncertain, and using common sense will help protect tourists during their stay in Japan.**

Sexual Assault

If you are a victim of sexual assault in Japan, it's essential to take immediate steps to protect your safety and seek help. First and foremost, if you are in immediate danger, **call the police at 110.** The police will respond quickly, and it's important to provide them with as much information as possible, including details about the incident, your location, and any information about the assailant.

Once you've ensured your immediate safety, you should seek medical attention. If you're able, go to a hospital as soon as possible to receive a medical examination. This **examination is crucial**, as it may collect

important evidence, such as DNA or physical trauma, that could be vital for any potential investigation. Even if you do not feel physically injured, it's advisable to have a doctor examine you for any internal injuries, as well as for potential sexually transmitted infections (STIs). Hospitals in Japan are equipped to handle cases of sexual assault, and medical professionals can guide you through the process.

When you are ready, you can file a report with the police. In Japan, reporting a crime like sexual assault is a sensitive and personal matter. While the authorities are generally professional, some survivors may feel uncomfortable or intimidated by the process, especially due to the cultural stigma surrounding sexual violence. Having a trusted friend, family member, or a professional support service present during the reporting process can help alleviate some of these feelings. The Japanese legal system is often criticized for its handling of sexual assault cases, especially regarding the investigation process, but **reporting the crime ensures there is an official record** and can help initiate the legal proceedings.

Victims of sexual assault in Japan also have access to support services. There are various NGOs and organizations that offer assistance to survivors, including counseling, emotional support, legal guidance, and referrals for medical care. One such organization is the **Rape Crisis Center** in Tokyo, which provides free services for victims of sexual violence, including legal advocacy, emotional counseling, and interpretation services for non-Japanese speakers. In addition, Japan has a number of **women's shelters** and hotlines available for those in need of a safe place or emotional support. These services can guide you through the complexities of the legal and recovery process, as well as help you understand your rights as a survivor.

If you are not comfortable or confident in speaking Japanese, many of these support organizations can provide translation or interpretation services to help you navigate the legal and medical systems. It's also a good idea to contact your embassy or consulate, as they can assist with language barriers and help you understand the local legal framework. They can also provide a list of English-speaking lawyers who specialize in sexual assault cases, should you require legal representation.

While navigating the aftermath of a sexual assault can be traumatic, it's essential to know that support is available. In Japan, many survivors find strength through counseling and therapy, which can help process the emotional, mental, and physical impact of the assault. Though Japan's legal and social systems regarding sexual violence can be challenging, seeking help and using available resources can assist in finding justice and healing.

 **General Questions**

1. *If I am a victim of a crime, can I legally be compensated?*
   Yes. In Japan, victims of crimes may be eligible for compensation, though the process can be complex. Under the **Criminal Injury Compensation Act**, the government provides financial assistance to victims of violent crimes to cover medical expenses, lost wages, and funeral costs if the victim is killed. This compensation is available even if the offender is not identified or cannot pay.

   If the perpetrator is caught and convicted, victims can seek **damages** through a civil lawsuit, though collecting these funds can be challenging, especially if the offender has limited assets. Victim support organizations also provide legal and financial guidance, helping victims navigate the compensation process. While compensation is possible, the process can be slow and the amounts may be limited, so seeking legal advice is recommended.

2. *What legal rights and protections do crime victims have in Japan during the trial process?* In Japan, crime victims have the right to participate in the trial, either by submitting statements or testifying. They are also entitled to be informed about the case's progress. Victims can seek restitution for costs like medical bills or funeral expenses. Additionally, victim support organizations offer legal and psychological assistance. However, critics note that the system could improve in terms of victim involvement and support during trials.

3. *How does Japan handle the protection of witnesses and victims during criminal trials?* In Japan, witness and victim protection is limited compared to other countries. While there is no formal witness protection program, victims of violent crimes may testify remotely or behind a screen to avoid direct contact with the defendant. For serious cases, police may offer protection, but the level of support varies. Critics argue that Japan's system needs improvement to better protect vulnerable witnesses and victims.

POLICE

POLICE

Overview[35]

The organizational framework of Japan's police force is primarily divided into two main entities: the **National Police Agency** (**NPA**) and the **Prefectural Police**. The **NPA** serves as the central coordinating body for the entire police system, developing policies and overseeing the operations of the prefectural police departments across the nation. At the national level, the NPA is supported by the National Public Safety Commission (NPSC), which ensures the political neutrality and effectiveness of the police. Local police operations are managed through 47 **Prefectural Police Departments**, each responsible for law enforcement in their respective prefectures. Although these departments function independently, they adhere to the policies and guidelines set by the NPA, ensuring unified law enforcement across the nation.[36]

Within each prefectural police department, various **specialized bureaus** and **divisions** address specific aspects of police work, such as traffic management, criminal investigations, community safety, and public security. This layered structure enables law enforcement to adapt to diverse local needs while maintaining coordination with national standards.

---

35 https://www.toolify.ai/ai-news/exploring-the-japanese-police-system-structure-roles-and-challenges-14276

36 https://www.npa.go.jp/english/Police_of_Japan/2020/poj2020_p2-7.pdf

As of recent data, the total number of police personnel in Japan was approximately 296,400, encompassing both the National Police Agency and the Prefectural Police. The Tokyo Metropolitan Police Department (MPD) had the highest concentration of police personnel, with about 43,500 employees.[37] The sheer size of the police force reflects Japan's commitment to maintaining public safety and responding effectively to criminal activity. Furthermore, the ratio of police officers to the population is about one officer per 556 citizens, demonstrating a considerable presence of law enforcement personnel. This staffing ratio is crucial in providing timely and effective responses to emergencies and criminal incidents, illustrating the importance placed on community safety.

The staffing of Japanese police forces is characterized by a systematic recruitment process that emphasizes merit and competency. The National Police Academy and various regional police schools conduct rigorous training for newly recruited officers, covering various aspects of law enforcement, including criminal law, investigation techniques, and community policing.

The hierarchy within the police ranks comprises nine levels, starting from Police Officer and progressing to the Superintendent General, who oversees the NPA Promotions within the police force are merit-based, often requiring candidates to pass relevant examinations.

Despite its extensive staffing, the Japanese police force faces challenges in recruitment, particularly in urban areas like Tokyo, where a noticeable decline in applicants has raised concerns about future personnel. Creative recruitment strategies, such as initiatives aimed at engaging younger generations, are being explored to ensure the continued strength of the police workforce.

---

37 https://www.statista.com/statistics/1178465/
japan-number-of-of-police-personnel-by-prefecture/

Police Response

The Japanese police force plays a critical role in **maintaining public order**, **ensuring safety**, and **preventing crime**. Their primary functions include investigating crimes, enforcing laws, managing traffic, and responding to emergencies. The police are also tasked with counterterrorism efforts, maintaining public order during large events, and providing disaster response in the event of natural catastrophes. **Community policing** is a cornerstone of the Japanese police system, with officers stationed at *koban* (police boxes) in neighborhoods to provide a visible presence and build trust with local residents.

One of the significant challenges facing the police in Japan is maintaining **low crime rates** while still addressing **emerging issues** such as **cybercrime**, **organized crime**, and **social unrest**. Japan's traditionally low crime rate has meant that the police have not had to deal with high levels of violent crime, but they must still focus on preventing non-violent crimes, such as fraud and drug offenses. Another challenge is addressing **public concerns about police conduct** and ensuring the proper treatment of suspects, especially given the controversies surrounding the **pretrial detention system** and the use of confessions obtained during interrogations.

There have been **ongoing reforms** within the police force aimed at improving its effectiveness and addressing these challenges. These include greater emphasis on **modernizing law enforcement technology** and improving investigative techniques, particularly in cybercrime and organized crime. Additionally, reforms are being made to better support **victims of domestic violence** and **sexual assault**, ensuring that officers are more sensitive and responsive to the needs of victims. Another key area of reform involves improving **police transparency** and addressing concerns about their interrogation methods, particularly the practice of holding suspects for extended periods without charge.

In recent years, Japan's police force has also been working on increasing **diversity** within its ranks to better reflect the country's changing demographics, including a growing foreign population. There is also a push to improve police **community engagement** to ensure greater public trust and cooperation.

Police and Community Relations

In Japan, the overall image of the police is **largely positive**, with the force viewed as **efficient, disciplined**, and **effective** in maintaining public order. The police are generally seen as trustworthy and dedicated to ensuring the safety of citizens, contributing to the country's reputation for being one of the safest in the world. The **community policing model**, with officers stationed at koban, fosters a visible, approachable police presence in neighborhoods, which helps build trust between law enforcement and the public. This community-based approach allows officers to develop close ties with local residents, who often view police officers not only as law enforcers but as part of their everyday environment.

There is also significant respect for the police's role in preventing crime, particularly violent crime, and their ability to manage emergency situations, including natural disasters and large public events. As a result, Japan consistently enjoys low crime rates, which contributes to the public's confidence in the police force.

However, there are some areas where the perception of the police can be more complex. One of the **main criticisms** is related to **police interrogation** practices. Concerns have been raised over the **pretrial detention system**, where suspects can be held for extended periods without charge, and over the reliance on confessions—sometimes obtained under duress—to secure convictions. These practices have garnered attention both domestically and internationally, with critics arguing that these methods can lead to miscarriages of justice, and there have been calls for reform in how suspects are treated during police investigations.

Police Use of Force

Police use of force in Japan is generally not seen as a major issue compared to other countries. The country's police force is known for its **discipline, restraint**, and **emphasis on de-escalation**. Japan has **one of the lowest crime rates in the world**, and **violent confrontations** between the police and civilians are **extremely rare**. The Japanese police operate under strict guidelines regarding the use of force, with an emphasis on proportionality—using force only when absolutely necessary and in a manner that is proportional to the threat posed.

However, there are occasional instances where the use of force by the police has raised concerns. In particular, issues can arise during arrests or crowd control, where the use of force may sometimes be questioned in terms of whether it was necessary or excessive. These instances are rare, but they can draw public attention, especially if they involve allegations of police brutality or excessive violence against specific groups, such as minorities, foreign nationals, or suspects in custody.

For instance, **Japan's interrogation methods** have been criticized internationally for their reliance on coercive tactics to obtain confessions, which can include prolonged detentions and aggressive questioning, although this is more an issue with investigative practices rather than physical violence. While there are some calls for greater oversight of police practices and better protections for individuals, particularly in cases of police custody and interrogations, these instances are exceptions rather than the rule. On the whole, Japan's police force enjoys a strong reputation for professionalism, and the use of force remains relatively infrequent and carefully controlled under the country's legal system.

 **Law of the Land True Story**[38]

In January 2024, a landmark lawsuit was filed in Japan by three foreign-born residents who accused the police of engaging in racial profiling during routine questioning. The plaintiffs, including an African American, a Pacific Islander, and a man of Pakistani descent, each alleged that they have been repeatedly targeted by police based on their ethnicity or appearance. They are seeking ¥3.3 million (about US$22,300) in compensation for the harassment they experienced.

---

38 https://www.gmanetwork.com/news/topstories/world/895740/
lawsuit-filed-over-everyday-racial-profiling-by-japan-police/story/)

One of the plaintiffs, Maurice, a U.S. citizen, claimed he had been questioned 16 or 17 times over the course of a decade in Japan, despite having lived there with his Japanese family. He described these encounters as an "everyday occurrence" and expressed frustration over the lack of accountability. Another plaintiff, Matthew, a Pacific Islander permanent resident, said he had been questioned about 100 times, which led him to become socially withdrawn.

This lawsuit is significant because it is the first of its kind in Japan, focusing specifically on racial profiling by law enforcement. Although Japan has seen an increase in immigration, foreign-born residents represent only 2.3 percent of the population, making the issue of racial discrimination more pronounced. Japan's National Police Agency (NPA) acknowledged past instances of inappropriate questioning but insisted there was no intent to discriminate. The lawsuit highlights growing concerns about how racial profiling impacts marginalized communities and calls for changes in police practices.

HOW TO GET LEGAL HELP IN JAPAN

HOW TO GET LEGAL HELP IN JAPAN

Available Resources[39]

If you are arrested in Japan, it is essential to act quickly to secure your rights and access appropriate legal representation. First, you should contact your **embassy or consulate**. The embassy will assist you by providing guidance on legal procedures, helping you find reliable legal representation, and offering consular services such as verifying your well-being. The embassy can also communicate with local authorities on your behalf and help ensure your rights are respected.

Finding reliable legal representation in Japan can be done through various channels. It is crucial to seek a **Japanese lawyer** who is familiar with the country's legal system because legal procedures and practices may differ from your home country.

 Your embassy can provide a list of recommended lawyers who speak English and have experience with foreign nationals. Such a list provided by the U.S. Embassy in Tokyo can be found at **https://jp.usembassy.gov/services/attorneys/tokyo-lawyers/**.

---

39 https://sumikawa.net/legal-services/when-you-are-arrested-in-japan/)

Additionally, the **Japan Federation of Bar Associations (JFBA)** is a reputable resource where you can find qualified lawyers specializing in criminal defense. You can also search for local legal aid services if you need help with fees. When selecting a lawyer, ensure that they have experience handling cases similar to yours and that they are fluent in a language you can communicate comfortably in, such as English. It is important to have a legal professional who understands both the intricacies of the Japanese justice system and your specific situation.

Legal Aid

In Japan, **foreign visitors are eligible for legal aid**, but there are certain criteria and limitations based on the specific circumstances of the case. Legal aid in Japan is designed to provide assistance to individuals who cannot afford to pay for legal representation and to ensure access to justice for everyone, including foreigners.

To qualify for legal aid in Japan, foreign visitors must meet specific **financial criteria**. Legal aid is generally available for individuals who cannot afford to hire a lawyer. The Japan Legal Support Center (*Hôritsu Sōdan Sentā*) determines eligibility based on the applicant's **income and assets**. The center assesses whether the applicant's financial situation is such that they cannot bear the cost of legal fees.

In addition to financial need, the **nature of the case** also plays a role. Legal aid is more likely to be provided for serious criminal cases, civil disputes involving significant stakes, or cases where the individual is in danger of facing unjust treatment.

Legal aid in Japan typically encompasses a **wide range of services** designed to support individuals during the legal process. This includes:

- **Legal advice:** Foreign visitors can receive consultations and legal guidance regarding their case.
- **Attorney representation:** Legal aid covers the cost of hiring a qualified lawyer who will represent the individual in court or during the investigative phase.

- **Court fees:** In certain circumstances, legal aid may cover court-related costs, such as filing fees or administrative costs related to the legal proceedings.

- **Interpretation and translation:** For non-Japanese speakers, legal aid may also provide access to **interpreters** or translations, especially for crucial legal documents or court hearings.

To apply for legal aid, foreign visitors must submit an application through the **Japan Legal Support Center** (*Hôritsu Sōdan Sentā*). The process involves providing details about one's financial situation and the nature of the legal issue. Applicants may also need to submit relevant documents that demonstrate their income, assets, and the details of the legal problem they are facing. It's important to note that legal aid may **not cover all types of cases**. For instance, certain minor infractions or civil matters may not qualify for legal assistance if they don't meet the criteria set by the Japan Legal Support Center.

Foreign Embassies in Japan

Foreign embassies and consulates in Japan play a crucial role in protecting and assisting their nationals, facilitating diplomatic relations, and offering a range of services to foreign residents and visitors. Their main functions are to represent the interests of their home country, provide consular services to their citizens, and promote cultural, trade, and economic ties between Japan and their home country.

Embassies and consulates can assist their nationals abroad, offering support during legal or emergency situations. They help with cases of arrest, missing persons, hospitalizations, deaths, and natural disasters, providing legal referrals, arranging for lawyers, and helping secure travel documents, like emergency passports. Embassies serve as the official representatives of their governments in Japan, fostering diplomatic relations, promoting trade, and supporting cultural and educational exchanges.

In times of crisis, embassies provide emergency support, including evacuation assistance and shelter, and help nationals navigate dangerous situations. They also offer notarial services, authenticate documents, and assist with registering life events like births, marriages, and deaths abroad.

Lastly, many embassies organize cultural events and educational fairs to promote their home country's culture and strengthen ties with Japan, fostering greater global understanding.

Most foreign embassies in Japan are concentrated in **Tokyo**, the capital city, which is the political and economic hub of the country. Tokyo is home to the Embassy of Japan and embassies of the majority of foreign nations. Diplomatic missions are typically located in the **Minato ward** (the district where many foreign embassies are situated) and other central areas of Tokyo.

In addition to the embassies, there are **consulates** in major cities throughout Japan, including **Osaka, Kyoto, Fukuoka**, and **Sapporo**, where smaller diplomatic or consular offices provide services to the local foreign community. Some countries with a significant population of expatriates or strong trade ties with Japan may have **multiple consulates** across the country, in addition to their embassy in Tokyo.

 A list of foreign embassies in Japan can be accessed at **https://www.mofa.go.jp/about/emb_cons/protocol/a-h. html**.

MEDICAL FACILITIES & HOSPITALS

MEDICAL FACILITIES & HOSPITALS

Overview

Japan's healthcare system is widely regarded as **one of the best in the world**, known for its high quality, accessibility, and affordability. The system operates under a **universal health insurance** model, which means that all residents, including foreigners who live in Japan for over a year, are required to have health insurance.

This system is primarily divided into two types: **employer-based insurance** for employees and their families, and a **public health insurance** system for self-employed individuals and retirees. The healthcare system is decentralized, with local governments responsible for administering public health insurance schemes. Healthcare services are delivered through a mix of public and private providers. **Public hospitals are government-funded** and often seen as **more affordable**, while **private hospitals** and clinics tend to offer **shorter wait times** and **more personalized care**. Both types of facilities are equipped with high-standard medical technologies and staffed by highly trained healthcare professionals.

Accessibility is a key strength of Japan's healthcare system. There are numerous clinics, hospitals, and specialized medical centers spread across the country, making healthcare services readily available in both urban and rural areas. The country has a relatively **low doctor-to-patient**

ratio, which ensures that patients receive quick attention and care when needed.

The quality of care is high, with Japan consistently ranking well in global health indicators, such as life expectancy, maternal and child health, and the treatment of chronic diseases. Japan's healthcare system is also known for its focus on preventive care, health screenings, and early detection of illnesses.

Affordability is another key advantage of Japan's healthcare system. Although healthcare can be expensive without insurance, the cost is **heavily subsidized through the public insurance system.** People typically pay around 30 percent of the medical costs, with the rest covered by their insurance. The costs for prescription medications, doctor's visits, and even surgeries are significantly lower than in many other developed countries. Moreover, Japan has a cap on the amount patients are required to pay out-of-pocket for high-cost medical treatments, ensuring that no one faces financial hardship due to medical expenses.

Visitors' Access to Healthcare in Japan

Visitors to Japan can access medical services, though the process can differ from what they are used to in their home countries. Visitors who are staying in Japan for a short period (less than a year) are generally not required to join Japan's national health insurance system. However, they can still receive medical care by paying out-of-pocket or using private travel insurance.

If visitors are not covered by any insurance, they will need to pay for medical services **out-of-pocket.** Japan's medical fees can be high, but they are typically lower than in many Western countries. The cost of consultations at general clinics typically ranges from ¥2,000 to ¥5,000 (US$15 to $35), while more specialized care or visits to hospitals may cost more. Visitors are advised to pay the bill directly after receiving treatment. For more expensive procedures, hospitals may request payment upfront or provide information on how to arrange for reimbursement if the visitor has travel insurance.

Many visitors opt for **travel insurance**, which often covers medical expenses for illnesses, injuries, and accidents while traveling abroad. This is especially useful if visitors do not have a local health plan. Travel insurance can also help cover the cost of hospitalization, medical procedures, medications, and even emergency medical evacuations, depending on the terms of the policy. It's essential to check that the insurance includes coverage for medical treatment in Japan, as not all policies may extend to international healthcare.

Language can be a significant challenge when seeking medical help in Japan, as most healthcare professionals speak Japanese, and **English proficiency is not widespread**, especially in smaller clinics or rural areas. However, major hospitals in large cities like Tokyo and Osaka often have English-speaking staff or interpreters available, particularly in international medical centers. Some clinics and hospitals also provide services for foreigners, offering bilingual signs and translating apps to help bridge the communication gap.

In cases where no English-speaking staff are available, visitors can bring along an interpreter or use a translation app, which can be helpful for general communication. However, for more serious conditions or emergencies, it's advisable to seek out hospitals that specialize in serving international patients, where assistance in multiple languages is more readily available.

Japanese Hospitals

Japan has a well-developed healthcare infrastructure, with a large number of hospitals and medical professionals across the country. As of recent data, Japan has approximately **8,500 hospitals**, including public, private, and specialized facilities. These hospitals are equipped with advanced medical technologies and provide a range of services, from general care to highly specialized treatments.[40]

---

40 https://cigs.canon/en/article/20210416_5736.html

The medical workforce in Japan is extensive, with over 300,000 licensed physicians in the country, or 26.1 doctors per 10,000 population. This provides a high doctor-to-patient ratio, contributing to the overall quality of healthcare in the country.[41]

Hospitals in Japan are predominantly **concentrated in urban areas**, particularly in major cities like **Tokyo, Osaka**, and **Yokohama**, where the majority of specialized care, advanced treatment, and cutting-edge medical research is conducted. Tokyo alone has hundreds of hospitals, including some of the best medical institutions in the country. Rural areas, while serviced by hospitals, generally have fewer and smaller medical facilities, which may limit access to highly specialized care.

Among the best hospitals in Japan are **The University of Tokyo Hospital**, a leading public institution known for its advanced research and specialized care, and **Keio University Hospital**, another prestigious public hospital that provides top-tier treatment in various medical fields. Private hospitals such as **St. Luke's International Hospital** and **Juntendo University Hospital** also stand out, offering high-quality care and specialized services. St. Luke's, in particular, is popular among foreign residents for its excellent patient care and multilingual services. These hospitals, well-equipped to handle the needs of foreign patients, represent just a fraction of Japan's medical facilities, which overall boast a high standard of care and some of the world's best medical professionals.

---

41 https://healthsystemsfacts.org/national-health-systems/bismarck-model/
japan/japan-health-system-personnel/

 **General Questions**

1. *What should you do if you feel unwell/sick in Japan?* If you feel unwell in Japan, for minor issues, visit a local pharmacy for over-the-counter remedies. For more serious symptoms, visit a hospital or clinic. Emergency care can be accessed through the nearest hospital's emergency room or by dialing **119** for an **ambulance.** If you have health insurance, make sure to bring your insurance card for coverage. Without insurance, you'll need to pay out-of-pocket, and medical costs can be high. Many hospitals in cities like Tokyo or Osaka have English-speaking staff, and you can also contact your embassy for assistance in finding English-speaking medical care.

2. *Are there American hospitals in Japan?* **Yes.** There are American-affiliated hospitals in Japan that cater to the needs of expatriates, including American citizens. One notable example is the **American Medical Center Japan** (**AMC**), located in **Minato, Tokyo**. AMC is a private clinic that provides healthcare services in English, specializing in offering comprehensive medical care, including general health check-ups, specialist consultations, and emergency services. Additionally, The **Tokyo American Club** (**TAC**) in Tokyo offers access to medical services, including a partnership with local hospitals and clinics for expats needing English-language care. While Japan doesn't have an "American hospital" in the traditional sense of a hospital solely for Americans, many hospitals in major cities like Tokyo and Osaka have international clinics or dedicated staff that provide services in English.

Insurance Guidance[42]

Foreign insurance plans are **generally accepted in Japan**, but it's advisable to check with your provider beforehand to confirm whether they have agreements with Japanese hospitals. If your plan doesn't directly cover you, you will need to pay out-of-pocket and file for reimbursement later.

The cost of medical services can vary. A typical **doctor's visit** may cost between **¥5,000 to ¥10,000 (about US$33 - $67)**, while an **emergency room visit** can range from **¥10,000 to ¥20,000 (about US$67- $136)** or more, depending on the severity of the case. The cost for a basic consultation can also vary depending on the clinic or hospital.

Payments for medical services are usually made directly at the hospital or clinic after treatment. Payments can be made in cash, or credit cards may be accepted at larger hospitals. Keep in mind that you may need to pay upfront and file a claim with your insurance later for reimbursement, unless your insurance directly covers the cost.

---

42 https://www.internations.org/japan-expats/guide/healthcare#)

DRIVING IN JAPAN

DRIVING IN JAPAN

Overview[43]

Driving in Japan offers a unique and efficient experience for those familiar with road rules and local customs. The country is renowned for its **excellent road infrastructure**, which is meticulously maintained and offers a seamless driving experience, whether on highways or rural roads. Japanese roads are **well-marked** and **organized**, with clear signage, though it's important to note that **many signs are in Japanese**, with English translations typically available along major routes. Urban roads are particularly well-kept, though rural areas may have narrow and winding roads. The highways, or "expressways," are wide and multi-lane, designed for quick travel between major cities. The expressway network is extensive, connecting almost every part of the country.

The driving experience itself is governed by a culture of discipline, where respect for traffic laws is ingrained in the population. One of the first things foreign drivers will notice is that **Japan follows the British system**, meaning **driving is on the left side** of the road, with steering wheels on the right side of the car. **Speed limits** are strictly enforced, with **urban areas** having a limit of around **40 km/h (25 mph)** and **highways** ranging from **80 to 120 km/h (50-70 mph)**, depending on the type of road. There's a strong emphasis on road safety, with everyone required

---

43   https://niconicorentacar.jp/driving-in-japan/
driving-in-japan-the-complete-guide-for-tourists-and-foreigners/

to wear seat belts, and using mobile phones while driving is prohibited unless a hands-free device is used. Perhaps one of the most important road safety features is Japan's incredibly strict stance on alcohol. The **legal blood alcohol limit** is set at **0.03 percent**, so it's advisable to avoid any alcohol consumption if planning to drive.

Another key safety aspect is the **priority given to pedestrians.** In Japan, pedestrians typically have the right of way at crosswalks, and drivers will always stop for them, which may be surprising for visitors from countries with different traffic rules. Drivers are also expected to signal every turn well in advance, as signaling is taken very seriously, and failure to do so can result in fines. Japanese drivers generally **avoid honking their horns**, using them only in situations where it's necessary for safety, as honking can be perceived as an aggressive act. When it comes to parking, Japan is very strict about where you can park. Illegal parking is swiftly dealt with, and vehicles may be towed without notice.

For foreign visitors, driving in Japan requires some preparation. To legally drive in Japan, you must have an **International Driving Permit (IDP)** along with your **original driver's license** from your home country. It's important to get an IDP in your home country before arriving in Japan, as it's not possible to obtain one once you're there. If you're renting a car, most rental agencies will provide you with the necessary documentation and offer insurance coverage options. While basic insurance is mandatory, it's highly recommended to purchase additional coverage if not included in the rental agreement.

When driving on expressways, you'll encounter **toll roads**, which are a significant part of the road network. Tolls are based on the distance traveled, and the **fees can vary**, though typically a long trip between cities like Tokyo and Osaka could cost several thousand yen in tolls. The most common way to pay for tolls is through the **Electronic Toll Collection (ETC)** system, which uses a small device installed in your vehicle to automatically pay tolls as you pass through toll gates. Many rental cars come equipped with an ETC card, which makes passing through tolls much quicker and more convenient. If you don't have an ETC card, you can **pay manually** at tollbooths using cash or credit card. Cash is still the most commonly accepted payment method, but many tollbooths also accept credit cards.

While driving in Japan can be a smooth and enjoyable experience, it's important to stay mindful of the local customs, traffic regulations, and payment methods for tolls. With the right preparation, foreign drivers can navigate Japan's roads with confidence and take full advantage of the country's superb infrastructure. Whether you're driving in the bustling cities or the more serene countryside, Japan offers a driving experience that's as efficient as it is orderly.

 ## Main Traffic Rules & Road Safety Tips

- **Driving side:** Left side of the road

- **Speed limits:**

  - **Urban areas:** 40 km/h (25 mph)

  - **Non-urban areas:** 50–60 km/h (31–37 mph)

  - **Highways:** 80–120 km/h (50–75 mph)

- **Traffic signals:** Standard red (stop), yellow (prepare to stop), and green (go); flashing yellow means proceed with caution; flashing red means stop and proceed if safe.

- **Seat belts:** Mandatory for all passengers in the vehicle, front and rear.

- **Alcohol:** Legal limit: 0.03 percent; it's safest to avoid alcohol completely when driving.

- **Mobile devices:** Prohibited unless using a hands-free system; no texting or talking on the phone while driving.

- **Toll roads:** Pay via Electronic Toll Collection (ETC) system, or manually with cash or credit card; tolls are based on distance traveled.

- **If stopped by police:** Present your passport, International Driving Permit (IDP), and original driver's license; be polite and follow instructions.

- **Road safety tips:**

  - Drive defensively and stay alert, especially in urban areas.

  - Yield to pedestrians at crosswalks.

  - Avoid illegal parking, particularly in urban areas.

  - Be cautious of cyclists and motorbikes on the road.

  - Watch for snow and ice in winter, especially in rural areas.

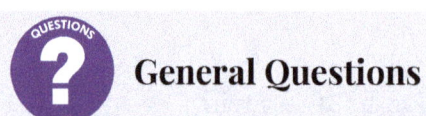 **General Questions**

1. *What is the age requirement for renting a car in Japan?*
   To rent a car in Japan, the **minimum age requirement** is typically **18 years old**. However, most rental companies will require drivers to be at least **21 years old** to rent a car without additional restrictions. If you're under 25, some rental agencies may charge a **young driver fee**, and in some cases, you may need to provide additional documentation or meet certain conditions.

   In addition to age, drivers must have held a valid driver's license for at least **one year**. Foreign drivers also need an **International Driving Permit (IDP)** in combination with their original driver's license if they are not from Japan.

2. ***What are the common driving customs and behaviors I should be aware of in Japan?*** When driving in Japan, politeness, patience, and respect for others are key. Always use your indicators when changing lanes or turning, as signaling is taken seriously. Speeding is uncommon, and violations result in heavy fines. Pedestrians have the right of way at crosswalks, so stop for them, and be cautious of cyclists. Overtake only from the right side, as the left lane is for faster traffic. Horns are used sparingly and only in emergencies. Always park in designated areas to avoid fines or towing. Japanese driving is quiet and reserved, with loud music or noise considered rude. Respect road signs, especially in school zones, and give way to buses, taxis, and emergency vehicles. By following these customs, you'll have a smooth and safe driving experience in Japan.

 ## Law of the Land Hypothetical

HYPOTHETICAL: *Mateo, a 28-year-old tourist from Spain, is visiting Japan for the first time. He decides to rent a car to drive from Osaka to Kyoto. While on the expressway, Mateo becomes distracted by the scenic views and misjudges a sharp curve near an exit. His car skids, hitting a guardrail and coming to a halt. Thankfully, Mateo is unharmed, and there are no other vehicles involved, but his rental car is badly damaged, and the traffic flow is disrupted. Mateo, unsure of what to do next, feels a bit panicked. He doesn't speak Japanese fluently and is worried about how this incident will affect his trip. What legal steps must Mateo take as a tourist involved in a traffic incident in Japan, especially since he's at fault for the accident?*

ANSWER: *First, Mateo should stop his car immediately. In Japan, leaving the scene of an accident is a serious offense, and failing to stop could result in criminal charges. He should check for any injuries, and even though he seems unharmed, he should call **119** to alert emergency services, ensuring any potential medical needs are addressed. Mateo should then call **110** to report the accident to the police, as all accidents,* *regardless of severity, must be reported. While waiting for the authorities, he should stay at the scene and remain composed.*

*When the police arrive, Mateo should provide his **driver's license, International Driving Permit (IDP), passport**, and **rental car agreement**. He should avoid admitting fault or apologizing, as the police will investigate and determine liability. Mateo should express concern for the situation without taking responsibility for the crash. Mateo should also contact the rental car company immediately to report the incident. The company will guide him on whether he needs to pay for damages or if his insurance will cover the costs. Mateo should also notify his travel insurance provider about the accident. If he has trouble understanding the process due to the language barrier, he should request an interpreter or contact his embassy for assistance.*

If Mateo is found at fault, he may be held responsible for damages to the rental car and any other property. Japan's traffic laws are strict, so following the correct procedures and cooperating with the authorities will help Mateo resolve the situation legally and minimize complications.

NUDE BEACHES & CLOTHING-OPTIONAL RESORTS

NUDE BEACHES & CLOTHING-OPTIONAL RESORTS

Overview

Nudism, as understood in many Western cultures, is **not widely practiced or culturally accepted** in Japan. Japan generally has a more **conservative approach to public nudity**, and social norms tend to favor modesty in public settings. While nudity itself is not inherently taboo in certain contexts (such as public baths or hot springs), the concept of **nudism** or **naturist culture** is not as established or accepted as it is in some other countries.

In Japan, public nudity is most commonly seen in the context of **onsen** (**hot springs**) or **sento** (**public baths**). Here, it is standard to bathe naked, but this is done in a private and communal setting where everyone is expected to follow strict hygiene practices before entering the baths. While this may appear similar to nudism, it is more about cultural tradition and cleanliness than an acceptance of social nudity or nudist lifestyles. These places are not intended for relaxation in the nude or for promoting nudism as a lifestyle.

Unlike some countries where there are designated nudist beaches, **Japan does not have official nudist beaches**. Nudity in public spaces, especially on beaches, is **generally not accepted**. People typically wear swimsuits at public beaches, and exposing oneself in a nudist manner could lead to **public indecency charges**. That said, there are very few secluded or private areas where people may engage in nude sunbathing, but these are not officially recognized or promoted. Some areas may allow people to be in the nude in secluded spots, but this would be more of an individual or private choice rather than a cultural norm.

There are no mainstream hotels or resorts in Japan that cater exclusively to **nudists** or **naturists**. Japanese accommodation, including resorts and ryokan (traditional inns), adhere to social norms where clothing is expected at all times, except in bathing or sleeping areas. There might be private hot spring resorts where you can bathe naked, but this is limited to the cultural practice of onsen bathing and does not extend to lifestyle nudism. In short, while Japan has a rich culture surrounding public bathing where nudity is expected in private and communal bath settings, **nudism as a lifestyle is not widely accepted or promoted.**

Legality and Safety[44]

Public nudity laws in Japan fall under the **Public Morals Law** (or **Public Decency Law**), which is designed to maintain public order and protect the general sense of modesty. Under this law, any form of **indecent exposure** or nudity in public spaces can be considered an offense. Public nudity or engaging in sexually suggestive acts in public spaces could lead to charges of indecent exposure (public indecency). The law prohibits actions that disturb public order or offend common moral standards, and nudity in public areas (like beaches, parks, or streets) typically falls under this category. Individuals caught engaging in public nudity may face **fines, arrest,** or **criminal charges for indecent exposure,** especially if the act is disruptive or sexually explicit. Foreign nationals could also face **deportation** or **bans from re-entering Japan.** Socially, public nudity can lead to significant stigma and damage to one's reputation.

In **private spaces,** such as homes or certain private resorts (like some ryokan with onsen), nudity is not regulated the same way. However, nudism settings do not exist on the same scale as in countries where nudism is a widely accepted lifestyle. Any organized nudist activities,

---

44 https://sandee.com/blog/nudism-laws-in-japan

such as **nude parties** or **nude events**, are rare and generally take place in private locations where all attendees consent.

 ## General Questions

1. *Is it okay to walk around topless at a secluded beach in Japan if there is nobody around?* **No.** It is not okay to walk around in the nude at a secluded beach in Japan. Even in secluded areas, public nudity is generally not accepted under Japanese law. If you are seen walking around nude, you could face legal consequences. It is important to respect local customs and laws by wearing appropriate swimwear in public spaces, including beaches.

2. *Could I be arrested if I'm walking around topless on a beach?* **Yes.** In Japan, you could potentially be arrested for walking around topless in public. Even if you are in a secluded area, the act of walking around topless could still be considered indecent exposure and a violation of public decency standards. While you might not face immediate arrest in all cases, you could be asked by local authorities to cover up or face legal consequences, including fines or arrest, depending on the situation.

 ## Law of the Land Hypothetical

HYPOTHETICAL: *Anna, a 30-year-old tourist from France, is visiting Japan and decides to spend her day at a remote beach near Kanagawa. Having previously enjoyed topless sunbathing in other countries, she assumes it's fine to do so in Japan, particularly since the beach is relatively empty. After lying on her towel for a while, a local police officer approaches and informs Anna that topless sunbathing is prohibited under Japanese law. The officer explains that public nudity, including*

toplessness, is considered a violation of the Public Morals Law and that such behavior can lead to legal consequences. Can Anna legally claim ignorance of the law to avoid penalties for topless sunbathing on a public beach in Japan?

ANSWER: *No. Anna cannot legally claim ignorance of the law as a defense in Japan. Public nudity, including topless sunbathing, is illegal in public spaces under Japan's Public Morals Law, and this law applies regardless of whether a person is aware of it. Even if Anna is unfamiliar with the law, she is still required to adhere to local customs and regulations. Ignorance of the law is not a valid excuse, and she could face fines or arrest for violating public decency standards. In Japan, cultural norms dictate that swimwear should be worn at all times on public beaches, and public nudity is not tolerated.*

UNUSUAL LAWS

UNUSUAL LAWS

Overview

Unusual laws can be fascinating glimpses into a culture's values and history. While most people are aware of common legal restrictions, it's often the strange and quirky laws that capture our attention. These regulations can range from the amusing to the absurd, reflecting the unique circumstances and traditions of a place. Whether they arise from historical events, societal norms, or simply peculiar local customs, unusual laws can provide insight into the quirks of human behavior and governance.

 **Japan's Unusual Laws and Associated Penalties**

Japan has a few unique and quirky laws that might surprise visitors. While the country is known for its orderly and respectful society, some of its legal regulations can seem unusual to those unfamiliar with the culture. Here are a few examples, along with the associated penalties for breaking these laws:

The "Kissing in Public" Law

Public displays of affection (PDA), like kissing or making out in public, are not common in Japan and are frowned upon. While it's not technically illegal to kiss in public, it is considered socially inappropriate and could lead to unwanted attention.

Penalties: While no legal penalty exists for kissing in public, engaging in excessive PDA might be met with social disapproval, fines in some rare cases (like in amusement parks or public places if it causes a disturbance), or the involvement of law enforcement if it disrupts public order.

The Tattoo Restriction

Tattoos in Japan have a long association with the *Yakuza* (Japanese organized crime), and because of this, many onsens, gyms, swimming pools, and public baths refuse entry to anyone with visible tattoos. While this is slowly changing, tattoos can still carry a social stigma in some areas.

Penalties: There are no legal penalties for having tattoos, but you might be refused service at certain establishments, such as spas or public baths. In some cases, you might be asked to cover your tattoos or even leave.

The "Dancing After Midnight" Ban

Until recently, Japan had a law that banned dancing after midnight. The **Entertainment Business Law of 1948** prohibited dancing in public places after midnight unless the establishment was licensed for late-night dancing. The law was originally enacted to control the rise of certain underground clubs.

Penalties: Breaking this law could result in hefty fines for businesses hosting illegal dance events or individuals caught dancing in unlicensed venues after midnight. The law was relaxed in 2015, but many establishments still must adhere to certain restrictions.

The "Flashing Headlights" Law

Flashing your headlights to signal another driver in Japan is illegal. In Japan, flashing your headlights is often seen as a sign of aggression or an attempt to force another driver to give way.

Penalties: This action can lead to fines or points on your driver's license. In some cases, it can even lead to more severe penalties if the flashing leads to accidents or road rage.

The "No Rude Gestures" Law

In Japan, making rude gestures or gestures like the "middle finger" is seen as extremely disrespectful. While not explicitly illegal, making such gestures in public or toward others can escalate into a legal issue if it leads to public disturbances.

Penalties: While making rude gestures might not always result in legal punishment, it can cause a disturbance of the peace or lead to a confrontation, which may result in fines, warnings, or police involvement if things escalate.

 **General Questions**

1. *Are there restrictions on the sale of certain foods in Japan, such as raw meat or fugu (pufferfish)?* **Yes**. Japan has strict regulations on the sale and preparation of certain foods, particularly raw items like *fugu* (pufferfish) and raw meat. Fugu is highly regulated, requiring chefs to be licensed to prepare it due to its potentially lethal toxins. Raw meat, especially dishes like *basashi* (raw horse meat), is subject to health and safety regulations, and its sale is restricted in some regions. Violating food safety laws can lead to severe penalties for businesses.

2. *Can you legally sleep in public spaces like trains or parks in Japan?* While it is not illegal to sleep in public spaces such as trains or parks in Japan, there are certain expectations and social norms to follow. In trains, it's common for people to nap, especially during long commutes, and it is generally accepted as long as it doesn't disturb others. Sleeping in parks is not illegal either, but doing so in a way that obstructs public pathways or causes discomfort to others could result in a warning or removal by authorities. In some cases, sleeping in public areas at night could also be seen as a sign of vagrancy, and individuals could be approached by police if it's deemed suspicious or disruptive.

3. *Is it illegal to take out your garbage too early in Japan?* **Yes.** In Japan, it is illegal to take out your garbage too early. Garbage collection days and times are strictly regulated in local neighborhoods to maintain cleanliness and public order. Each neighborhood has specific schedules for when trash can be put out and taking it out before the designated time is considered a violation. This can result in fines and, in some cases, social repercussions from neighbors who place a high value on adhering to these regulations. The law reflects Japan's strong commitment to maintaining a clean and orderly environment in both public and private spaces.

 **Law of the Land Hypothetical**

HYPOTHETICAL: *Maria, a tourist from Italy, buys a snack at a convenience store in Osaka. She pays with a ¥1,000 bill (approximately US$6.71) for a ¥450 snack (approximately US$3.02), and the cashier mistakenly gives her ¥1,000 (approximately US$6.71) in change instead of ¥550 (approximately US$3.69). Maria notices the mistake but decides to return the extra ¥500 (approximately US$3.36) to the cashier. The cashier thanks her but later reports the incident to the police.*

ANSWER: *It is illegal to knowingly keep excessive change returned by a cashier in Japan, as this is considered fraud and violates the cultural principles of honesty and integrity. Those who knowingly keep extra change could face fines or imprisonment as a result. However, Maria would most likely not face any legal consequences since she returned the extra change as soon as she noticed the mistake. She acted in good faith and avoided any fraudulent intent. Japanese law focuses on deliberate fraud, so her immediate correction would prevent any charges.*

TRAVELING SAFELY

TRAVELING SAFELY

Ladies Traveling Solo

Japan is widely regarded as one of the safest countries in the world for travelers. It consistently **ranks high in global safety** indices due to its **low crime rates, efficient infrastructure,** and **high standard of living.** Visitors often comment on the country's **cleanliness, polite people,** and **overall sense of order.** Violent crime is rare, and petty crimes like pickpocketing are even less common compared to other countries. In addition, public transportation is incredibly safe, even at night, and there is a strong sense of community responsibility in ensuring public safety.

Japan is generally considered a **very safe destination for solo female travelers.** Many women feel comfortable navigating the country alone, whether it's exploring the cities, enjoying nature, or visiting cultural sites. Japanese society places high value on respect and courtesy, which contributes to a relatively low occurrence of harassment or unwanted attention. Women traveling alone will find that the public transport system is safe, and most accommodations are welcoming and well-secured.

Certain districts in larger cities might have higher risks of nightlife-related incidents, which include:

- **Roppongi (Tokyo):** Known for its vibrant nightlife scene, Roppongi has some areas where scams or overcharging can occur, especially involving foreigners. While it's generally safe, it's recommended to avoid wandering alone late at night in less crowded areas of the district.

- **Kabukicho (Shinjuku, Tokyo):** Kabukicho is Tokyo's entertainment and red-light district, and while it is a popular area with plenty of restaurants, bars, and nightclubs, it can be chaotic and sometimes dangerous late at night. It's best to stay in well-lit, busy areas and be cautious about entering establishments with questionable reputations.

- **Osaka's Namba District:** Namba is a busy commercial area with plenty of shops, restaurants, and entertainment venues. However, some of the more obscure alleys and establishments may cater to less-than-friendly crowds or involve scams. Avoid wandering into quieter, less well-lit alleys late at night.

- **Famous Nightlife Areas (in general):** While areas like Shibuya and Harajuku in Tokyo or Dotonbori in Osaka are usually safe, any nightlife district after hours can have increased risks of drunken behavior, petty theft, or being approached by aggressive individuals trying to lure tourists into bars or clubs. It's best to stay alert and be cautious.

Overall, Japan remains one of the safest countries for female travelers, with the vast majority of experiences being pleasant and trouble-free. The few areas mentioned are exceptions, and in general, it's always wise to exercise the usual caution while traveling anywhere.

As with any destination, solo female travelers should still take **basic safety precautions.** It's important to stay aware of your surroundings, especially when traveling in unfamiliar areas. Avoid isolated or poorly lit streets late at night, and stick to well-populated, busy places. If using public transportation, be cautious when on late-night trains, as these can sometimes attract rowdy behavior, although such incidents are rare. It's also a good idea to have a charged phone with you at all times, and when in doubt, don't hesitate to ask for help from staff or locals who are usually very polite and helpful. Always have a map or know your route to avoid getting lost, and if staying in a hotel or hostel, opt for accommodations with good security measures, such as 24-hour reception or key card access.

Traveling as a Family[45]

Traveling as a family in Japan offers an exciting and enriching experience. The country is well-known for its family-friendly atmosphere and its excellent infrastructure, making it easy to navigate with children. Japan's **public transportation system**, especially its trains and subways, is **efficient** and **well-connected**, making it simple to explore both busy cities like Tokyo and more serene areas. However, it's important to keep in mind that rush hours can be crowded, so it's wise to **plan travel times carefully**. Many train stations offer elevators and escalators, and there are designated family cars on trains, which makes traveling with young children or strollers more convenient. It's also helpful to teach children basic etiquette, such as keeping quiet on trains and not blocking walkways.

When it comes to accommodations, **most hotels** in Japan are **very accommodating to families**. Many offer amenities like cribs, child-sized slippers, and highchairs, though it's always a good idea to confirm these details in advance. Japan is also known for its **child-friendly restaurants**, some of which offer kids' menus or even dedicated play areas to keep children entertained while parents enjoy a meal. As for **attractions**, Japan is home to several world-famous theme parks, such as Disneyland Tokyo and Universal Studios Japan, as well as a variety of cultural and historical sites that offer engaging experiences for families. These places tend to be **family-centric**, with plenty of **kid-friendly activities**. However, be prepared for long queues during peak travel seasons. It's helpful to plan your day to maximize fun and minimize frustration.

In addition to being aware of the logistics, it's also important to instill in children an **understanding of Japan's cultural norms**. The country places a strong emphasis on politeness and respect, and children should be taught to speak softly in public, wait patiently in line, and avoid running or being disruptive in public spaces. Understanding and practicing these local customs can help families blend in and enjoy a smoother experience.

---

45 https://www.japan.travel/en/ca/inspiration/
travelling-in-japan-with-kids/)

When it comes to health and safety, traveling with children requires a few extra precautions. First and foremost, ensure that you have **travel health insurance** that covers medical care abroad. Japan has an excellent healthcare system, but medical care can be expensive for those without coverage. It's important to familiarize yourself with Japan's **emergency numbers: 110 for police** and **119 for medical emergencies.** Keeping these on hand, as well as a list of nearby hospitals or clinics, can provide peace of mind in case of an emergency.

In addition to health insurance, staying **hydrated** and protecting children from the sun is crucial, especially in the hot summer months. Japan can experience **intense heat**, so it's important to make sure children wear sunscreen, hats, and appropriate clothing to prevent sunburn. Always carry a refillable water bottle, as tap water in Japan is safe to drink. During the hottest parts of the day, it's advisable to take breaks in shaded areas to keep cool. When it comes to food, Japan is known for its safety and cleanliness in food preparation. However, if your child has food allergies, it's essential to check food labels, especially with packaged goods, and be mindful of street food, ensuring it's prepared in hygienic conditions. If your child has a sensitive stomach, it's also good to ease them into trying unfamiliar foods.

In busy cities, where **crowds can be overwhelming**, it's crucial to keep a close eye on children. In popular tourist areas, it's easy for kids to wander off, so ensuring they have some form of identification—whether it's a name tag or contact information—can be a helpful precaution. For added security, consider using a **child safety wristband** or a **GPS tracker.** Japan is a very safe country, but it's always best to stay cautious, especially in crowded spaces.

Finally, be mindful of your family's energy levels. While there's so much to see and do, it's important to schedule downtime for rest and naps to avoid overwhelming younger children. Many public places like parks and department store lounges have quiet spaces where families can relax and recharge. In the event of illness or injury, Japan's pharmacies and hospitals are well-equipped to handle a wide range of common ailments. If your child needs specific medication, it's best to bring it along, along with any necessary prescriptions. If you're not familiar with Japanese, translation apps can help when communicating with medical staff.

Advice for All Travelers

Japan is often regarded as one of the safest and most welcoming countries for travelers, but there are still a few things to keep in mind to ensure a smooth and respectful visit. While the country is known for its polite society and well-organized systems, understanding and adapting to local customs, being mindful of social etiquette, and following certain practical tips can help visitors avoid misunderstandings and enjoy their trip to the fullest. From navigating public transportation to interacting with locals, a little awareness can go a long way in enhancing your experience in Japan.

Remember that **cultural etiquette** plays a significant role in daily life. Japanese society values respect, humility, and consideration for others. It's important to be mindful of local customs, such as bowing when greeting someone, speaking quietly in public spaces, and not tipping in restaurants, as tipping can be seen as rude. Public behavior, including avoiding loud conversations or phone calls in trains and public spaces, is expected.

Another area to be cautious about is **public transportation during rush hours** when trains and subways can become very crowded, particularly in cities like Tokyo. It's advisable to avoid traveling during these times if possible, or to be prepared for packed trains. It's also important to follow the rules, such as queuing for trains and giving up seats for the elderly, pregnant women, and people with disabilities.

Crossing streets is another thing to pay attention to. Although Japan has a reputation for being orderly, not all pedestrians always follow the rules. While traffic lights and pedestrian crossings are well-marked, you should still be cautious when walking, as some locals might jaywalk, especially in less busy areas. Always look both ways, even when crossing at designated crossings.

Cash handling in Japan is also something to consider. While Japan is a relatively cash-based society, especially in rural areas, you will find that most businesses in cities accept credit cards. However, small shops, markets, and some restaurants may only accept cash, so it's important to always have enough yen on hand. ATMs in convenience stores often accept international cards, but fees may apply.

If you're planning to visit *onsen* (**hot springs**), it's important to follow the bathing etiquette. Most onsens require that guests thoroughly wash and rinse their bodies before entering the communal hot baths, and tattoos are sometimes frowned upon in traditional onsens, though this is changing in some places. It's best to check in advance whether tattoos are allowed at certain facilities.

When it comes to **food** in Japan, be cautious with street food if you have a sensitive stomach, especially if you're unfamiliar with the ingredients or preparation methods. It's always safer to eat at established places or look for food stalls that appear busy, as this often indicates a higher standard of hygiene.

Lastly, while Japan is one of the safest countries in the world, always be aware of your surroundings, particularly in crowded or tourist-heavy areas. Although violent crime is rare, petty theft can occur in tourist hotspots. Keeping your belongings secure, especially in crowded places, is always a good practice.

 **Do's and Don'ts While in Japan**

When visiting Japan, understanding and respecting local customs can greatly enhance your experience. The country places a strong emphasis on politeness, cleanliness, and social harmony, so being mindful of cultural norms is key. Whether it's how you greet someone or how you behave in public spaces, small gestures can go a long way in showing respect for Japanese traditions. Here are some Do's and Don'ts while in Japan:

- **Do** always **bow** when greeting someone. Bowing is a traditional form of greeting and shows respect in Japanese culture, especially in formal settings.

- **Don't tip**; tipping **is not customary in Japan.** Instead of tipping, showing respect through polite language and gestures is appreciated. Tipping can sometimes be seen as rude or confusing.

- **Do take off your shoes** when entering homes, temples, or certain accommodations like ryokan inns and onsens. It is customary in Japan to remove your shoes to maintain cleanliness.

- **Don't point directly at people or things.** Pointing is considered impolite in Japan. Use your whole hand to gesture or gently point with your chin if necessary.

- **Do queue up** and wait in line. Japan is known for its orderly lines at train stations, elevators, and other public spaces. It's a social expectation to wait your turn.

- **Don't speak loudly in public.** In Japan, loud conversations in public places, especially on public transportation, are frowned upon. It's best to speak quietly to avoid disturbing others.

- **Do use both hands when handing over money or gifts.** This is a sign of respect in Japan, particularly in formal settings or with elders.

- **Don't engage in public displays of affection.** Kissing or hugging in public is seen as inappropriate in Japan. It's better to keep affectionate gestures private.

CHAPTER 22
TOURIST TAXATION

TOURIST TAXATION

Overview

Tourism plays a significant role in Japan's broader economy, contributing billions of dollars annually and supporting a wide range of industries, including hospitality, transportation, retail, and entertainment. In recent years, Japan has seen a **steady increase in international visitors**, especially leading up to events like the 2020 Tokyo Olympics (delayed to 2021). Tourism not only boosts local businesses but also helps promote regional development and job creation, particularly in less-visited rural areas.

Tourist taxes, such as the "Japan Tourism Tax" and the "Accommodation Tax" in certain cities, are a **crucial source of funding for public services and infrastructure**. The taxes collected from tourists are used to enhance and maintain essential services that benefit both locals and visitors, including transportation networks, waste management, security, and public amenities. These funds are also used to improve tourism infrastructure, like airports, train stations, and tourist information centers, ensuring that Japan remains an attractive, safe, and sustainable destination for future travelers.

Tourist Taxes in Japan[46]

Japan has implemented several types of tourist taxes to help support its infrastructure and public services, especially as the number of international visitors continues to rise. These taxes primarily target visitors staying in accommodations or entering the country. They are designed to ensure tourism's economic benefits are reinvested into maintaining and improving the country's tourism infrastructure.

One of the most well-known tourist taxes is the **Accommodation Tax**, which is levied on travelers staying at hotels, inns, or other accommodations in certain cities. The rate varies depending on the accommodation type and the city but generally ranges from **¥100 to ¥500 (about US$0.70-3.50) per person, per night**. Major cities like Tokyo, Osaka, Kyoto, and Sapporo charge this tax, with the amount typically being higher for more expensive accommodations. For instance, staying at a luxury hotel might incur a higher tax rate compared to budget options.

Another key tax is the **Japan Tourism Tax**, which was introduced in 2019. This tax is a fixed fee of **¥1,000 (about US$6.70) per person** and applies to international travelers departing Japan. It's collected when purchasing airline tickets for international flights and is generally included in the price of the ticket. The Japan Tourism Tax aims to help finance improvements to tourism infrastructure, such as enhancing airports, creating tourism information centers, and supporting disaster recovery efforts in tourism-dependent areas.

These taxes are generally simple to pay and are automatically included in your travel-related expenses. For accommodation tax, it's added directly to your hotel or lodging bill, while the Japan Tourism Tax is bundled into the cost of your flight ticket. This system ensures that tourists contribute to the upkeep and enhancement of the very infrastructure they rely on during their visit.

---

46 https://www.itt-show.jp/tokyo/en-gb/press/latest-news/travel-taxes-in-japan.html

In addition to the Accommodation Tax and the Japan Tourism Tax, there are a few other **regional fees and charges** tourists may encounter. Some local governments impose small fees for **admission to popular attractions**, temples, or museums, helping to maintain cultural sites and tourism infrastructure. Certain **national and regional parks** may also charge **entrance fees** to support conservation and maintenance efforts. Though not a formal "tourist tax," Japan's **consumption tax** of 10 percent applies to most goods and services, including food and souvenirs, with tax-free shopping available for foreign visitors making qualifying purchases. All these taxes and fees contribute to maintaining Japan's infrastructure and services for both residents and tourists.

 **Law of the Land Hypothetical**

HYPOTHETICAL: *Laura and her family, including her two young children (aged 4 and 6), are visiting Japan from the United Kingdom. They stay at a mid-range hotel in Kyoto for three nights. Upon check-out, Laura is surprised to see an additional Accommodation Tax charge for ¥500 (about US$3.36) per adult, but there is no charge for her children. Laura is unsure if this is correct and asks the hotel staff whether the Accommodation Tax should apply to her children. Are small children subject to the Accommodation Tax in Japan, and how is it calculated for families?*

ANSWER: *In this case, the hotel is applying the Accommodation Tax correctly. Typically, Accommodation Taxes in Japan are charged only for persons who require their own bed or sleep in separate accommodations. Since Laura's children were sharing a bed with their parents and did not incur any additional charges for the room, the Accommodation Tax does not apply to them. The tax is calculated based on the cost of the accommodation per person, so children who stay for free with their parents are generally exempt from the charge.*

LONG-TERM STAYS

- Overview
- Long-Term Visas
- General Questions
- Law of the Land Hypothetical
- Takeaways

CHAPTER 23
LONG-TERM STAYS

Overview

As of 2023, Japan recorded approximately 3.4 million foreign nationals living in the country, which constitutes about 2.7 percent of the total population. This marks a notable increase from previous years. The number of foreign residents has steadily grown, with registered long-term foreign residents reaching a record high of approximately 3.31 million by mid-2024, reflecting a growth of 5.8 percent from the previous year. This trend highlights an increasing acceptance of foreign nationals within Japanese society and indicates the vital role they play in addressing labor shortages.[47] Japan has seen an influx of long-term residents from countries like China, Korea, Brazil, the Philippines, and the United States, among others. Many foreigners come to Japan on work visas, while others are students, spouses of Japanese citizens, or permanent residents. The government has also made efforts in recent years to attract skilled labor through specific visa categories, such as the "Highly Skilled Professional" visa, which allows foreigners with advanced skills to live and work in Japan for extended periods.

People choose to stay long-term in Japan for various reasons, ranging from work and education opportunities to a deep appreciation of the country's culture and lifestyle. One of the main draws is Japan's **high**

---

47   https://www.japantimes.co.jp/news/2024/10/18/japan/society/
     foreign-residents-figures/

quality of life, with **excellent public transportation, healthcare, and safety**. Additionally, the country offers a **fascinating blend of modern living and traditional culture**, appealing to those interested in both the convenience of urban life and the serenity of rural areas. For many, the opportunity to experience Japan's rich cultural history, such as visiting temples, festivals, and natural landmarks, is a significant motivating factor. Additionally, Japan has a **thriving job market**, especially in industries like **technology, engineering, teaching**, and **tourism**, making it an attractive destination for expatriates. The allure of **Japan's food, fashion**, and **overall lifestyle** also makes it a desirable place for long-term residence.

When it comes to the **best regions** or **cities for long-term stays**, it depends on personal preferences and priorities. **Tokyo**, the capital city, is an obvious choice for those seeking a bustling urban environment with access to numerous job opportunities, vibrant cultural events, shopping districts, and entertainment. It's ideal for people who thrive in a fast-paced, cosmopolitan setting. **Osaka** is another popular city for long-term stays due to its friendly atmosphere, rich culinary culture, and less hectic pace compared to Tokyo, while still offering many of the conveniences of a major city. For those looking for a more relaxed lifestyle, **Kyoto** offers a historic, tranquil setting surrounded by natural beauty, making it a great option for people interested in Japan's cultural heritage and slower pace of life. Meanwhile, for those seeking more affordable options or wanting to experience Japan outside the major urban centers, cities like **Fukuoka** in Kyushu or **Sapporo** in Hokkaido are gaining popularity due to their lower cost of living, good job prospects, and access to nature. Each region offers unique advantages, and the best location for a long-term stay ultimately depends on one's lifestyle preferences, career goals, and desire for urban or rural experiences.

Living Costs in Japan

Living costs in Japan **vary** depending on the city, lifestyle, and personal choices, but it's generally considered **moderately expensive**, especially compared to Western countries like the USA. Major cities like Tokyo and Osaka have higher living costs, particularly for rent and dining, while rural areas are more affordable.

Housing Costs:

Rent is the largest expense, with small apartments in Tokyo and Osaka typically ranging from ¥80,000 to ¥150,000 per month (around US$550 to $1,030), depending on location. Suburban and rural areas offer more affordable options, starting at around ¥50,000 to ¥80,000 (US$340 to $550). Initial rental costs can be high due to key money, deposits, and agency fees.

- **Utilities:** Monthly utility costs (electricity, gas, water) are usually between ¥10,000 and ¥20,000 (US$70 to $140). Internet and mobile phone plans are affordable, with internet costing ¥3,000 to ¥5,000 (US$20 to $35) per month and mobile plans starting at ¥3,000 to ¥7,000 (US$20 to $50).

- **Food Costs:** Grocery shopping can range from ¥30,000 to ¥50,000 (US$210 to $340) per month. Dining out at casual restaurants costs ¥500 to ¥1,500 (US$3.50 to $10.50) per meal, while mid-range restaurants may charge ¥2,000 to ¥5,000 (US$14 to $35). Imported goods and Western-style restaurants tend to be more expensive.

- **Transportation Costs:** Public transportation is efficient and affordable. A monthly pass costs ¥10,000 to ¥15,000 (US$70 to $100), with single metro rides costing ¥200-¥500 (US$1.40 to $3.50). Prepaid cards like Suica or Pasmo are commonly used for convenience.

- **Healthcare Costs:** Japan's healthcare system is affordable, with monthly premiums for National Health Insurance (NHI) ranging from ¥10,000 to ¥30,000 (US$70 to $210) based on income. Patients generally pay 30 percent of medical costs, with the government covering the rest.

Healthcare for Long-Term Visitors

In terms of healthcare, Japan offers some of the **best medical services in the world**. Foreign long-term residents are generally required to enroll in the **National Health Insurance (NHI)** system, which provides access to comprehensive medical care at an affordable rate. With the NHI, residents typically pay about 30 percent of medical expenses, while the government covers the remaining 70 percent. For those working in Japan, employer-based health insurance may also be available, offering similar benefits. Additionally, foreigners who have lived in Japan for more than a year are eligible for the **Social Insurance System**, which includes both health insurance and pension contributions. While healthcare in Japan is highly accessible and affordable, it's important for foreign residents to ensure they are properly enrolled in the system to avoid high out-of-pocket expenses.

Housing Options for Long-Term Stays

Housing options for long-term stays in Japan vary depending on the region and the **type of accommodation** desired. In urban areas like Tokyo and Osaka, expatriates typically opt for apartments, ranging from smaller one-room units (often referred to as **1K or 1DK**) to larger multi-bedroom apartments. Rent can be high in major cities, especially in central districts, but more affordable options exist farther from the city center. **Shared apartments** or **guesthouses** are also popular among foreigners, offering lower rent and opportunities to meet other people. For those who prefer more traditional living, options like **share houses** or renting a **tatami room** in a shared house may also be available. Rural areas tend to offer more affordable housing, but they may come with fewer amenities and longer distances to urban centers.

Transportation Options

Transportation in Japan is world-renowned for its efficiency, reliability, and extensive coverage. In cities, **public transportation** is the most popular option for getting around. Japan's **train system** is extensive and well-connected, with fast **Shinkansen (bullet trains)** offering quick travel between cities and local trains serving urban and suburban areas. For daily commuting, **subways, trains**, and **buses** are the go-to methods of transportation. In major cities like Tokyo and Osaka, getting a **suica** or **pasmo card** (prepaid transportation cards) makes it easy to pay for travel without the need for cash. **Bicycles** are also commonly used, particularly for short distances or in residential areas. While owning a car is possible, it is often not necessary in large cities due to excellent public transport, and parking can be expensive. In more rural areas, however, a car may be needed due to less frequent public transport options.

Language Considerations

For long-term visitors to Japan, learning Japanese is highly recommended due to the language barrier. While English is understood in some tourist areas and among younger generations, it's not widely spoken in daily life, especially outside major cities. Understanding basic Japanese, including reading hiragana, katakana, and kanji, can significantly ease tasks like shopping, navigating transportation, and interacting with locals. Japanese language skills are also important for professional settings, as most workplaces expect fluency in the language. Additionally, many official documents and government services are available only in Japanese, so language proficiency can make dealing with bureaucracy smoother. Overall, learning Japanese helps visitors better integrate into Japanese society, both socially and professionally.

Long-Term Visas[48]

Japan offers several types of long-term visas for foreign residents, each with specific requirements and purposes. These visas typically allow individuals to stay in Japan for periods ranging from one year to several years, depending on the visa type.

- **Work Visas:** One of the most common long-term visas, issued for various professional fields such as engineering, teaching, business, and research. To qualify, applicants generally need to have a job offer from a Japanese company, meet certain educational or professional qualifications, and demonstrate proficiency in the required field. Common work visa types include **Engineer/Specialist in Humanities/International Services**, **Intra-Company Transferee**, and **Skilled Worker** visas.

- **Student Visas:** Foreign nationals wishing to study in Japan can apply for a student visa, which allows them to stay for the duration of their course or program. This visa generally requires proof of enrollment in a Japanese educational institution and proof of financial ability to support oneself during the stay. Student visa holders

---

48 https://matcha-jp.com/en/9945

can also work part-time, but there are restrictions on the number of hours they can work.

- **Spouse or Dependent Visas:** Individuals married to Japanese citizens or long-term residents can apply for a **spouse visa**, which allows them to live and work in Japan. Similarly, foreign nationals who are dependents of someone with a work visa can apply for a **dependent visa**. The requirements for these visas are typically straightforward, but applicants may need to provide proof of the relationship or family dependency.

- **Permanent Residency:** After living in Japan for several years (usually 10 years for most foreigners, but as few as 1-3 years for those with certain types of work or family connections), foreign residents can apply for **permanent residency**. This visa allows individuals to live and work in Japan indefinitely without needing to renew their visa. The application process for permanent residency is stringent and involves an extensive background check, proof of financial stability, and a demonstration of integration into Japanese society.

- **Highly Skilled Professional Visa:** This visa is designed to attract foreign workers with advanced skills in areas like engineering, business, and research. Applicants must meet specific criteria, such as having a high level of education or work experience. Those who qualify can receive favorable treatment, such as a fast-tracked path to permanent residency.

- **Working Holiday Visas:** Available to nationals of countries that have a **working holiday agreement** with Japan, this visa allows young people (typically between 18-30 years old) to travel, work, and study in Japan for up to a year. The primary purpose of this visa is to allow cultural exchange and tourism while allowing individuals to support themselves through temporary work.

 For more information on visas, requirements and fees, please visit Japan's Ministry of Foreign Affairs website at **https://www.mofa.go.jp/j_info/visit/visa/index.html.**

? General Questions

1. *If I want to stay in Japan for long-term and work, should I apply for a work permit before arriving in Japan?* **Yes.** If you want to stay in Japan for the long term and work, you should apply for a work visa before arriving. Japan requires foreign nationals to have a valid work visa to legally work in the country. The process typically involves securing a job offer from a Japanese employer who will sponsor your visa application. After receiving the job offer, your employer will submit the necessary paperwork to the Japanese immigration office, and you will need to provide documents such as proof of qualifications, work experience, and sometimes language proficiency. It's important to note that working without a valid visa in Japan is illegal and can lead to serious consequences, including deportation and a ban from re-entering Japan. Therefore, ensure that your work visa is approved before you arrive to avoid any legal issues.

2. *I am American. Can I retire to Japan?* Japan does not offer a specific retirement visa for foreign nationals, so Americans looking to retire in Japan will need to explore alternative visa options. One common route is through a **long-term stay visa**, such as a **spouse visa** if married to a Japanese citizen, or a **dependent visa** if financially supported by a family member with a valid work visa.

Alternatively, retirees may apply for a **temporary visitor visa** (which allows stays up to 90 days), but this does not permit long-term residency or work. While some long-term stay options exist, such as **permanent residency** (typically after living in Japan for at least 10 years), there is no direct path for retirement unless the individual meets specific conditions or has other ties to Japan (such as family or substantial financial means). For those seeking retirement in Japan, it's also essential to show **proof of financial stability**, as retirees are generally expected to support themselves without working. This could involve demonstrating sufficient savings or income from pensions or investments.

 **Law of the Land Hypothetical**

HYPOTHETICAL: *Emily, a 40-year-old American, has been living in Japan on a work visa for the past three years. Recently, she decided to switch careers and pursue a new job in a completely different industry. Her current employer is not able to transfer her to the new role, and she plans to resign from her current job. Can Emily remain in Japan after resigning from her current job while waiting for her new work visa application to be processed?*

ANSWER: *Emily can stay in Japan for a limited time after resigning from her job, but she cannot work until her new work visa is approved. Under Japanese immigration laws, a work visa is tied to a specific employer. If she leaves her job, her work visa becomes invalid, and she would need to apply for a new visa under the new employer. While she waits for the new visa application to be processed, she can stay in Japan under a designated activities visa (which allows temporary residence while awaiting a new work visa), but she cannot engage in any work until the visa is granted. The process of transitioning between employers and visa types may take several weeks, so it's crucial for Emily to ensure she applies for the new visa promptly and adheres to the conditions of her stay. If she overstays or works without the proper visa, she could face legal penalties or be deported.*

 **Takeaways**

- Japan's foreign resident population has grown substantially, largely due to labor shortages and increased immigration.
- Major cities like Tokyo, Osaka, and Kyoto attract long-term residents for their lifestyle, culture, and job opportunities, while rural areas offer more affordable options.

- Japan can be expensive, especially in cities like Tokyo, but rural areas offer lower rent and living expenses. Daily costs like utilities and food are manageable compared to the U.S.

- Foreigners in Japan must enroll in National Health Insurance, covering 70 percent of medical costs, with employers providing additional coverage for workers.

- Japan offers various long-term visas, including work, student, and spouse visas. Permanent residency is available after several years, with strict requirements.

-

CHAPTER 24
CIVIL LITIGATION

CIVIL LITIGATION

Overview

Civil litigation provides a mechanism for resolving disputes, ensuring that travelers have a way to seek justice if legal issues arise while visiting another country. It helps them understand their rights and obligations under local laws, which may differ from those in their home country. The civil litigation system offers a formal process for addressing conflicts, such as contract disputes or personal injury claims, and can deter unfair practices by encouraging businesses to comply with legal standards. It also allows individuals to seek financial recourse for damages or losses and helps protect them from potential exploitation by local entities. Overall, understanding civil litigation enhances a visitor's experience and safety while traveling.

Personal Injury Claims and Compensation Law

In Japan, personal injury claims and compensation are rooted in civil law, specifically **tort law**, which addresses cases where an individual suffers harm due to the wrongful actions—either intentional or negligent—of another party. The legal basis for personal injury claims is found in the Civil Code, particularly **Article 709**, which states that anyone who intentionally or negligently causes harm to another person is liable for damages. In order to bring a successful claim, the injured party must prove that the responsible party's actions directly led to the injury.

Personal injury claims in Japan can arise in a variety of situations, including **traffic accidents, workplace accidents, medical malpractice, slip and fall incidents,** or **injuries caused by defective products.** In each case, the injured person needs to show that the harm was caused either by negligence or, in certain cases, intentional misconduct.

When an injury occurs, there are several important steps that the injured party must take to protect their right to compensation. First, it is essential to **seek medical treatment** right away. Prompt medical attention not only ensures that the injury is treated properly but also creates important documentation of the injury's extent, which is necessary for proving the case later on. If possible, **gathering evidence** at the scene of the injury is also important. For instance, in traffic accidents, taking photographs of the damage, collecting witness contact information, and documenting the circumstances of the accident can help build a strong case. In workplace accidents, it is critical to report the injury to the employer immediately, as this documentation is necessary for both insurance claims and potential legal action. In all cases, it is advisable to **consult with a lawyer** who specializes in personal injury law to navigate the process, understand one's rights, and ensure proper legal steps are followed.

Once the claim process begins, the **calculation of damages** in Japan involves several key components. **Medical expenses** are usually the most straightforward type of compensation, covering the cost of treatment, surgery, rehabilitation, and any future medical care required as a result of the injury. If the injury causes the victim to miss work, compensation for **lost wages** is also included. This amount is typically calculated based on the victim's average earnings and the time they are unable to work. In cases of long-term or permanent disability, the victim may be entitled to compensation for the **loss of future income.** Additionally, Japan provides compensation for **pain and suffering**, known as *isharyō*. This type of compensation addresses the emotional and physical distress caused by the injury. Pain and suffering compensation can vary greatly depending on the severity of the injury, its impact on the victim's quality of life, and the degree of negligence involved. In the case of a fatal injury, the victim's family can claim **funeral expenses and other related costs.** The overall amount of compensation is determined by the combination of these factors, with the severity of the injury playing a central role in the final calculation.

Insurance plays a significant role in personal injury claims in Japan. In cases of traffic accidents, drivers are required by law to have **liability insurance**, which typically covers damages caused to other parties in the event of an accident. If the at-fault driver has insurance, the injured party can usually claim compensation through that insurance company. If the at-fault driver is uninsured or underinsured, the injured party can pursue the responsible party directly through the legal system. In the case of workplace injuries, Japan's **Industrial Accident Compensation Insurance Act** provides compensation for employees who are injured while on the job. This insurance is mandatory and ensures that workers are compensated for medical costs, lost wages, and even death benefits for their families. In product liability cases or medical malpractice claims, manufacturers or medical providers may also have insurance coverage, allowing victims to claim compensation from the responsible party's insurer.

Legal fees in personal injury cases in Japan typically follow a **contingency fee** structure. This means that lawyers charge a percentage of the compensation awarded or settled, rather than an hourly fee or a flat rate. This arrangement allows individuals to pursue claims even if they do not have the financial means to pay upfront legal fees. The percentage usually ranges from **10 percent to 30 percent of the total settlement or award**. However, there are other costs that may arise during the legal process. If the case proceeds to court, there will be **court fees**, which include filing fees, expert witness fees, and the costs associated with obtaining medical records or other forms of evidence. In some cases, if the claim is resolved through mediation or arbitration rather than court proceedings, there may be **administrative fees** involved, though these are generally lower than court costs. If the defendant is found not liable or the case is dismissed, the injured party may be responsible for some of the legal costs, including the defendant's attorney fees, depending on the specifics of the case.

How to File a Civil Claim

Filing a civil claim in Japan is a structured process governed by the Civil Code and Civil Procedure Code. To file a claim, the plaintiff must have a **legal interest** in the matter, which means they must be directly affected by the issue and have valid legal grounds such as a breach of contract, tort (personal injury or property damage), or other civil matters. The claim must also fall within the **statute of limitations**, which typically ranges from three to ten years, depending on the type of claim. **Jurisdiction** must be correct, meaning the court must be able to address the claim, usually based on where the defendant resides or where the incident occurred.

Civil claims in Japan can cover a range of issues, such as contract disputes, personal injury (tort claims), property disputes, family law (divorce, custody), employment issues (unfair dismissal, wages), or debt recovery. To file, the plaintiff must submit a **complaint**, which outlines the facts of the case and the remedy sought. This is accompanied by **evidence** like contracts, medical reports, witness statements, and any physical evidence supporting the claim. **Identification documents** are required, as well as proof of payment for the **filing fee**, which depends on the value of the claim. If represented by a lawyer, their details must be included, and a power of attorney is needed if a third party is filing the claim.

Civil claims are generally **filed in a district court**, which handles most types of civil disputes. For family-related issues like divorce or custody, the case should be filed in a **family court**. Smaller claims, typically under 1.4 million yen, can be filed in a **summary court**, which offers a quicker, more cost-effective process. In complex cases, claims may be filed in higher district courts in cities like Tokyo or Osaka. Filing in the correct court is crucial to avoid delays or rejection of the claim. With the right documentation and guidance, the process is manageable, though legal advice is recommended to ensure proper procedure is followed.

Service of Documents

In Japan, the service of process in civil litigation is governed by the Code of Civil Procedure, which outlines specific rules and procedures for notifying individuals about legal actions against them. Service is typically handled by the **court execution officer**, with a court clerk managing the affairs related to service. Documents are usually served by **postal mail** or by a **court execution officer**. A court clerk may also personally serve a party involved in a case, and once service is completed, the person responsible for the delivery prepares a report detailing the service process and submits it to the court. Service is generally made at the recipient's domicile, residence, or business office. If these locations are unknown or service is not possible, documents may be delivered to the recipient's workplace, or to someone living with or working for the recipient.

The law does not differentiate between foreign and domestic companies in terms of service, and for individuals outside of Japan, the court can commission service through the relevant foreign authorities or the Japanese diplomatic mission in that country. Japan is a party to the **Hague Service Convention** and the **Convention on Civil Procedure**, so service to individuals in member countries follows these conventions.

In cases where service is impossible or the recipient's address is unknown, **service by publication** is used. This involves posting a notice in the court's public area or on the court's website if the service is done electronically. The government has been working on integrating more IT into court procedures, such as e-filing and electronic service of process. Starting in 2020, Japan's courts began implementing virtual proceedings, and plans are in place to allow e-filing and email service of complaints.

Statute of Limitations[49]

In Japan, the statute of limitations for civil suits is governed by the Civil Code, and the **length of the limitation period varies depending on the type of claim being made.** For most **general claims**, such as breach of contract or property damage, the statute of limitations is **typically 10 years** from the date the cause of action arises. However, for **certain specific claims**, such as personal injury or damage claims arising from torts (wrongful acts), the limitation period is generally **three years** from the date the plaintiff becomes aware of the damage and the identity of the responsible party. In cases where the **injury or damage is not immediately apparent**, the statute of limitations can be extended to **up to 20 years** from the occurrence of the incident. Claims related to **unpaid debts** or other financial obligations generally have a limitation period of **five years**.

Several factors can affect the length of the statute of limitations. For example, the period can be **paused or suspended** in certain circumstances, such as when the **defendant is temporarily unavailable** (e.g., when they are abroad or incapacitated) or when there is a **legal incapacity** on the part of the plaintiff (such as minors or individuals under guardianship). Additionally, the statute of limitations can be **interrupted or "reset"** if the defendant acknowledges the claim, such as through making partial payment on a debt or offering a written acknowledgment of liability. Such actions can reset the clock on the limitation period, effectively extending the time the plaintiff has to file a suit.

If a civil suit is filed after the statute of limitations has **expired**, the defendant has the right to raise the expiration of the limitation period as a defense. This is known as the "statute of limitations defense," and if the court determines that the suit is time-barred, it will typically **dismiss the claim**. However, in certain situations, the defendant may waive this defense, allowing the case to proceed even if the statute of limitations has expired. Additionally, there are exceptions that can extend or suspend the statute of limitations. For instance, in cases involving **fraud**

---

49 https://www.dlapiperrealworld.com/law/index.
    html?t=construction&s=liability&c=JP

or concealment of the cause of action, the limitation period may be **extended** until the plaintiff discovers the fraud, or in cases involving **minors**, the limitation period may be **suspended** until they reach the age of majority.

 ## Getting Married in Japan

Getting married in Japan involves specific legal requirements that both Japanese citizens and foreign nationals must meet. To get married legally in Japan, couples must submit an **application for marriage registration** (*kon'in todoke*) at the local municipal office. The legal process does not require a ceremony, though couples can choose to have one later. **For foreign nationals**, the process is similar, but they must provide **additional documentation** to confirm their eligibility. Both parties need to be **at least 18 years old** to marry, as Japan raised the minimum legal age for marriage to 18 for both men and women in April 2022. This is an important change from the previous law, which allowed women to marry at 16 with parental consent. Additionally, neither party can be married to someone else, and they must be mentally capable of entering into a marriage.

To apply for a marriage license, several documents are required. Japanese citizens need to submit their family register (*koseki tohon*) to prove their identity and eligibility. Foreign nationals must provide a **valid passport** and a **certificate of no impediment to marriage** (*kon'in yonin sho*), which is issued by their home country's embassy or consulate. The certificate confirms that the foreign national is legally able to marry under the laws of their home country. The process for obtaining a marriage license is straightforward, and couples must complete the marriage registration form at the local ward office, sign it, and submit it with the required documents. Once submitted, the local office will review the application and issue the marriage license. The registration process itself can take a **few days to a week**, depending on the office and the completeness of the paperwork.

Regarding ceremonies, Japan does not require a specific type of ceremony to validate the marriage. A **civil ceremony**, which is typically a straightforward legal procedure at the **municipal office**, is the most common method of marriage. Couples can choose to have a religious ceremony afterward, but it is not necessary for the legal recognition of the marriage. Many couples opt for a formal celebration or a Shinto, Christian, or Buddhist ceremony, but these do not carry any legal weight. After the marriage is registered, the couple will receive a **marriage certificate**. This document is used to prove the marriage and is typically required for changing a name, applying for spousal visas, or dealing with legal matters like taxes or inheritance. The marriage is officially recorded in the Japanese family register (koseki), which is a government document that records the family relationships of Japanese citizens. The registration of the marriage ensures that it is legally recognized within Japan.

The **cost** of getting married in Japan can vary depending on the municipality, but the fees for submitting the marriage registration are generally minimal, often around a few thousand yen (¥1,000 is approximately US$6.80). The fees for holding a ceremony, whether civil or religious, can be much higher, depending on the location and the type of ceremony.

Couples should be aware that **Japan does not automatically recognize foreign marriages for foreign nationals unless the marriage is registered with the Japanese authorities**. If one of the spouses is a foreign national, they must submit the necessary documents to the local municipal office for the marriage to be officially recorded in Japan. Additionally, Japan is a signatory to various international conventions, including the **Hague Convention on the Civil Aspects of International Child Abduction**, which may affect international recognition of the marriage in cases of child custody or divorce. Couples planning to live abroad or wishing to ensure their marriage is recognized in their home countries should consult with their respective embassies to ensure proper registration and recognition of their marriage both in Japan and internationally.

 **Law of the Land Hypothetical**

HYPOTHETICAL: *John, a U.S. citizen, is working in Japan on a temporary assignment. While walking to work, he slips on a wet surface in front of a store and suffers significant injuries, including a fractured leg. After receiving medical treatment, he discovers that the wet surface was caused by the store's negligence. There was no warning sign or barricade to alert pedestrians of the hazard. John wants to file a personal injury claim against the store for compensation. What is the statute of limitations for John's personal injury claim, and does the fact that several months have passed affect his ability to file the claim in Japan?*

ANSWER: *In Japan, the statute of limitations for personal injury claims is typically three years from the date the injured party becomes aware of both the injury and the identity of the responsible party. In John's case, since he was injured several months ago, the crucial factor will be when he first became aware of the store's negligence. If he was aware of the cause of the accident at the time of the injury, the three-year statute of limitations would start from that point. However, if he only recently learned that the store was negligent (for example, through an investigation or expert opinion), the clock may start from the date he became aware of this fact.*

It is also important to note that if John can demonstrate that he had not been able to reasonably discover the cause of the accident until recently (such as waiting for a medical evaluation or investigating the incident), the statute of limitations might be extended. However, if more than three years have passed since the injury occurred, and John has not yet filed his claim, he may face challenges as the store could raise the statute of limitations as a defense, potentially leading to the dismissal of his claim.

John should consult with a Japanese personal injury lawyer promptly to evaluate the situation and determine the best course of action. If the claim is filed within the appropriate time frame, he may be entitled to compensation for medical expenses, lost wages, and pain and suffering.

OTHER THINGS TO KNOW

CHAPTER 25

OTHER THINGS TO KNOW

Tourists and Street Hustling

Street hustling in Japan is generally **less common** compared to some other countries, but it does exist, particularly in areas with high concentrations of tourists. Street hustlers typically engage in **persistent and high-pressure sales tactics**, offering goods or services that seem too good to be true. Their behavior often involves approaching unsuspecting tourists with **unsolicited offers**, trying to create a sense of urgency or exclusivity, and often being very persistent in persuading tourists to make immediate purchases or commitments.

The goods and services commonly offered by street hustlers in Japan range from **counterfeit or low-quality electronics**, such as fake smartphones, to **knockoff designer clothing and accessories.** Some hustlers may also offer "exclusive" or "VIP" access to nightclubs, bars, or restaurants that are either overpriced or non-existent. Additionally, tourists may be offered **"special deals" for tours or other services** that turn out to be substandard or entirely fraudulent.

Street hustling is most prevalent in **major tourist hubs** like Tokyo's **Shibuya, Shinjuku**, and **Roppongi** districts, as well as in other large cities such as **Osaka** and **Kyoto.** These areas see heavy foot traffic from both local residents and international visitors, making them prime targets for hustlers looking to exploit tourists who may be unfamiliar with the local environment or wary of scams.

Local authorities and tourism organizations in Japan are aware of the issue and have taken measures to address street hustling. Tourism boards, local police, and information centers provide warnings and guidance for tourists about common scams and how to avoid them. In some tourist-heavy districts, law enforcement officers or specially assigned tourist police help monitor the situation and intervene when necessary. These measures are part of broader efforts to protect tourists and maintain Japan's reputation as a safe and welcoming destination.

Safety Concerns and Practical Tips

Interactions with street hustlers in Japan, while generally not as dangerous as in some other countries, still pose safety concerns. One major issue is the risk of financial loss due to scams, where tourists may be persuaded to pay for goods or services that are either fake, substandard, or non-existent. These hustlers often prey on unfamiliarity, targeting tourists who are not aware of the local market prices or who are unsure of local customs. Additionally, aggressive hustlers who persistently try to convince or follow tourists may cause psychological stress, making the tourist feel unsafe or uncomfortable. In some cases, street hustlers may also engage in overcharging for items or services, leading to a financial loss.

To protect themselves, tourists in Japan should take a few **precautionary measures**. First, they should be cautious when approached by strangers in busy tourist areas. It is often best to **politely decline unsolicited offers** and walk away without engaging further. If a tourist feels pressured or uncomfortable, it's important to stay calm, maintain a firm but polite demeanor, and **avoid making a purchase or commitment on the spot**. Tourists should also be aware of common scams, such as counterfeit goods or overpriced tickets, and do research beforehand to know typical prices for goods or services they are interested in. Having a **general understanding of the local pricing and market conditions** can help tourists avoid falling for fraudulent deals.

Local customs and behaviors can also help tourists navigate interactions with street hustlers. In Japan, it is **important to maintain politeness**

and respect, even in uncomfortable situations. Avoid raising your voice or reacting aggressively, as Japanese culture values calmness and composure. If someone is persistently pushing a service or item, it's perfectly acceptable to ignore them or walk away without feeling obligated to engage. In Japan, **being direct yet respectful is a social norm**, so tourists should not feel guilty about declining offers firmly and politely. Additionally, tourists should keep an eye on their surroundings and be aware of people following them or crowding them in tight spaces. **Staying aware** and being assertive in maintaining personal space can go a long way in avoiding unwanted interactions.

For tourists who feel harassed or scammed by street hustlers, several resources are available for reporting such incidents. Japan has a well-established network for tourist support, with tourist information centers in major cities offering assistance. These centers can help tourists report scams or harassment and provide guidance on the next steps. In cases where a scam involves significant financial loss, tourists can contact local law enforcement or the nearest embassy for support. The **Japan National Tourism Organization (JNTO)** also offers a tourist hotline where travelers can report any issues they encounter, including scams or aggressive street hustling. Local police stations, especially in tourist areas, often have English-speaking officers who can assist if a more formal complaint is necessary.

 ## In the Event of Death

In the unfortunate event that someone traveling with you dies while in Japan, it is important to stay calm and follow the necessary procedures. The first step is to **notify local authorities**, such as the police or emergency services, so that they can investigate the cause of death and confirm the circumstances. In Japan, the police are typically involved in such cases, especially if the death was unexpected or occurred under unusual circumstances. The authorities will provide guidance on the next steps and will issue an official death certificate once they have completed their investigation.

The **local embassy or consulate** can play a key role in helping you navigate the situation. They can assist with administrative tasks, such as issuing a death certificate, arranging for the repatriation of the body, and liaising with local authorities and funeral services. Embassies are also helpful in providing advice on the legal and cultural aspects of handling a death in Japan. Additionally, consular officials can help notify the deceased's family members and offer advice on funeral arrangements or legal matters, including inheritance and insurance claims. Embassies typically have a list of local funeral homes and transport companies that specialize in repatriating remains, making it easier for families to coordinate the process from abroad.

Handling the deceased's remains in Japan involves several legal and logistical steps. If the death was natural and no foul play is suspected, the family or traveling companions must **contact a local funeral home**. These companies are experienced in preparing the body for burial or cremation, which is the most common practice in Japan. If the family wishes to bring the body back to their home country, they must arrange for embalming, which is required for international transport of human remains. The funeral home will help with this process and prepare the necessary paperwork, including the death certificate and permits required for repatriation. Additionally, a medical certificate stating the cause of death and confirming that the body is safe to transport may be needed.

When bringing a body home, families should be aware that the **repatriation process** can be complex and expensive. The cost can vary depending on the distance, the funeral home services required, and the specific regulations of the destination country. It is important to consult with the embassy or consulate to ensure all legal requirements are met. Insurance coverage, if available, may help cover the costs of repatriation, so checking with the deceased's travel or life insurance provider is crucial. The consulate can assist in coordinating the paperwork and contacting the necessary authorities in both Japan and the home country to ensure a smooth and respectful process.

Experiencing Financial Hardship

Experiencing financial hardship while traveling in Japan can occur for a variety of reasons, such as **unforeseen emergencies, theft, losing a credit card, or mismanaging funds.** Some tourists may also find themselves in financial difficulty due to the **high cost of living** in major cities like Tokyo and Kyoto, where accommodation, food, and transportation can add up quickly. Additionally, language barriers can sometimes lead to miscommunications that result in unexpected expenses. In more serious cases, **accidents, illnesses, or unplanned medical expenses** can further strain finances.

If a tourist is running out of money or in need of financial assistance, the first step is to calmly assess the situation. If they have lost their wallet or credit cards, it is essential to **report the theft or loss** to the local police immediately. The police can provide a report, which may be necessary for insurance claims or to freeze credit cards. In many cases, embassies or consulates can assist with emergency funds, offering temporary loans or helping to facilitate contact with family or friends back home for money transfers. Tourists should also **contact their bank or credit card company** to inform them of the issue, as some institutions provide emergency cash services or the ability to transfer funds to local branches.

Japan has several **resources** and **support systems** in place to help travelers facing financial difficulties. Most major banks have international branches or ATMs that accept foreign cards, allowing travelers to access emergency funds from home. Additionally, money transfer services such as Western Union or international wire transfers are available at post offices and some convenience stores, making it easy to receive financial support from friends or family. Some hotels or hostels may also offer short-term credit or assistance in helping travelers contact their embassies. For tourists with travel insurance, the insurance company may be able to assist with emergency loans or reimbursements for specific situations, such as medical expenses or travel-related losses. In extreme cases, tourists can contact the **Japanese Red Cross** or **other charitable organizations**, which sometimes offer support for travelers in distress.

QUICK REFERENCE GUIDE

- Quick Chapter References to Important Topics

QUICK REFERENCE GUIDE

Crime in Japan

Are there particular areas I should avoid as a tourist?

Yes. Japan is generally safe for tourists, but areas like Kabukicho in Tokyo and certain nightlife districts in Osaka may have higher risks of scams or aggressive hustlers. Outdoor enthusiasts should be cautious in mountainous regions during typhoon or rainy seasons due to natural disaster risks. Some parts of Fukushima remain restricted due to radiation from the 2011 disaster. Overall, Japan is safe, and with awareness, tourists can avoid trouble and enjoy their visit. *For more details, see Chapter 3.*

Drug Offenses

Is the possession of marijuana legal?

No. Marijuana is classified as a controlled substance, and its possession, use, or trafficking is strictly prohibited under the Cannabis Control Law. Those caught with marijuana can face severe penalties, including imprisonment and fines, even for small quantities. Japan has a zero-tolerance policy for drug offenses, and penalties are particularly harsh compared to many other countries.

Is the possession of cocaine legal?

No. Cocaine is illegal under Japan's Narcotics and Psychotropics Control Law. Possession of any amount of cocaine can result in serious legal consequences, including long prison sentences. Japan enforces strict drug laws, and tourists or residents caught with illegal drugs can face severe punishment, including deportation for foreigners. *For more details, see Chapter 4.*

Alcohol-Related Offenses

What is the legal drinking age?

In Japan, the **legal drinking age is 20 years old.** Individuals under 20 are prohibited from purchasing, consuming, or possessing alcohol.

What is the legal blood alcohol limit to drive?

The legal blood alcohol concentration (BAC) limit for drivers in Japan is **0.03 percent.** This is a very low threshold, and penalties for driving under the influence are strict. Even small amounts of alcohol can result in heavy fines, license suspension, and potential imprisonment. Japan enforces zero-tolerance for drinking and driving, and the penalties are severe for those caught over the legal limit. *For more details, see Chapter 5.*

Firearm & Ammunition Offenses

Can I possess a gun or ammunition?

No. In Japan, firearm and ammunition possession is highly restricted and generally prohibited for civilians. Only licensed hunters or sport shooters can possess firearms, with a rigorous application process involving background checks, psychological evaluations, and secure storage requirements. Unauthorized possession of firearms or ammunition can lead to severe penalties, including imprisonment.

What are the penalties for possessing a firearm illegally in Japan?

> The penalties for possessing a firearm illegally in Japan are severe. Individuals caught with an unlicensed firearm can face **up to 10 years** in prison and **significant fines**. Additionally, possession of illegal firearms can lead to long-term imprisonment and deportation for foreign nationals. *For more details, see Chapter 6.*

Prostitution

Is prostitution legal?

> **No.** Prostitution is **illegal** in Japan under the Prostitution Prevention Law. While sexual services for money are prohibited, some adult entertainment businesses, like "soaplands," operate legally as long as they don't involve direct sexual acts. Soliciting or engaging in prostitution can lead to fines and imprisonment. *For more details, see Chapter 7.*

LGBTQ

Is homosexuality legal?

> **Yes**. Homosexuality is **legal** in Japan. There are no laws that criminalize same-sex relationships or activities.

Are same-sex public displays of affection legal and socially acceptable?

> While same-sex public displays of affection are **not illegal**, they can be considered **culturally sensitive** in Japan. Public affection, in general, is less common in Japan compared to many Western countries, and same-sex couples may face some social stigma in more conservative areas. However, there are no specific laws prohibiting such displays. *For more details, see Chapter 8.*

Arrested in Japan

Would I be entitled to bail if I'm arrested?

In Japan, bail is **possible**, but it is **not always granted** immediately. The decision to grant bail depends on factors such as the severity of the crime, the risk of flight, and the potential for tampering with evidence. In some cases, bail may be denied, especially for more serious crimes. If bail is granted, it typically involves a financial guarantee.

Will a lawyer be provided to me if I cannot afford one?

Yes. If you cannot afford a lawyer, Japan offers a **public defender** system. A lawyer will be appointed for you, though this typically occurs after the police interrogation phase. Legal aid may also be available for those who meet certain financial criteria, ensuring that all individuals have access to legal representation. *For more details, see Chapter 10.*

Helping a Friend or Relative Imprisoned in Japan

Can I send money to a friend or relative imprisoned in Japan?

Yes. You can send money to a prisoner in Japan, but it must be done through bank transfers or the prison's designated counter. Direct cash shipments are not allowed. It's best to contact the specific prison for detailed instructions.

Can I remain in Japan upon release from prison or jail after my sentence is complete?

Yes. You can remain in Japan after completing your sentence, but this depends on your visa status. If you were in Japan on a valid visa, it may be canceled upon your release, and you may need to apply for a new visa to stay. If you are not a Japanese citizen, immigration authorities will typically assess whether you should be allowed to remain in the country, and in some cases, you may be deported. It's important to clarify your immigration status with the relevant authorities before your release. *For more details, see Chapter 12.*

Crime Victim Assistance

Can a victim of a crime be legally compensated?

Yes. A victim of a crime in Japan can be legally compensated. Compensation may come from the perpetrator, depending on the outcome of the case, or through a government program known as the **Crime Victims' Compensation Act**. This provides financial assistance for medical expenses, lost wages, and pain and suffering caused by the crime.

How can a foreigner in Japan report a crime they are a victim of?

A foreigner in Japan can report a crime they are a victim of by visiting the nearest police station (koban) or calling the emergency number, which is **110** for immediate police assistance. Foreigners may also file a report in writing if they are not comfortable speaking Japanese. Many police stations in major cities have personnel who can communicate in English, and embassies can also assist with translation and navigating the legal process. *For more details, see Chapter 14.*

U.S. Consulate Assistance

Are there any limitations to the consulate assistance I can receive while in Japan?

Yes. While consulates and embassies in Japan can offer essential assistance to foreign nationals, their help is not unlimited. Consular support typically includes providing emergency travel documents, legal advice, and helping you contact family or friends. However, they cannot intervene in legal matters, such as representing you in court or influencing the outcome of legal proceedings. Additionally, consular staff cannot pay fines, settle debts, or provide financial aid (except in exceptional cases like emergency repatriation). *For more details, see Chapter 14.*

Police

Is there an official police force?

> **Yes.** Japan has an official police force known as the National Police Agency (NPA). The NPA oversees police activities throughout the country, including regional police departments. Japan's police are responsible for maintaining public order, preventing crime, and investigating offenses. *For more details, see Chapter 15.*

How to Get Legal Help in Japan

Is there a resource in Japan to find legal representation?

> **Yes.** There are resources in Japan to find legal representation. The **Japan Federation of Bar Associations (JFBA)** operates a lawyer referral service, and individuals can search for attorneys based on their needs or location.

Is there free legal representation assistance for foreign visitors?

> **Yes.** Free legal representation assistance is available in Japan for certain individuals, including foreign visitors. Local Legal Aid services (*Hōmu Sōdan*) provide free legal assistance to those who meet specific financial criteria, and they may assist foreigners in legal matters, including criminal cases or civil disputes.

Does the U.S. Embassy in Japan provide a list of local attorneys that speak English?

> **Yes.** Many foreign embassies provide a list of local attorneys who speak English. Embassies typically maintain contacts with local legal professionals and can guide foreign nationals in finding appropriate legal help, especially in urgent matters. *For more details, see Chapter 16.*

Foreign Embassies in Japan

Are there foreign embassies in Japan?

Yes. There are foreign embassies in Japan. Most countries have diplomatic missions in Tokyo, Japan's capital, and some may also have consulates in other major cities such as Osaka, Kyoto, or Fukuoka.

Is there a website to locate embassies in Japan?

Yes. There is a website to locate embassies in Japan. The Ministry of Foreign Affairs of Japan provides a list of foreign embassies and consulates on its website. You can also find embassy contact information, including addresses and phone numbers, through various international websites like **https://embassy-finder.com** or the specific embassy websites themselves. *For more details, see Chapter 16.*

Medical Facilities & Hospitals

Is there a number I can call for ambulance and fire emergencies?

Yes. In Japan, the emergency number for both ambulances and fire emergencies is **119**.

If I am injured while on vacation in Japan, are there hospitals that are recommended for tourists?

Yes. If you are injured while on vacation in Japan, there are hospitals that are tourist-friendly, particularly in major cities like Tokyo, Osaka, and Kyoto. Many hospitals in these areas have English-speaking staff or provide assistance to foreign tourists. Well-known hospitals that cater to international visitors include St. Luke's International Hospital in Tokyo, The University of Tokyo Hospital in Tokyo, Osaka University Hospital in Osaka, and Kyoto University Hospital in Kyoto. You can also contact your embassy or consulate for assistance in locating a hospital or medical facility with English-speaking staff. *For more details, see Chapter 17.*

Driving in Japan

Which side of the road do I drive on?

In Japan, you drive on the left side of the road.

Can I use my driver's license from my home country to drive in Japan?

Yes. To drive in Japan, you can use your home country's driver's license for a short period (usually up to one year) if it is accompanied by an International Driving Permit (IDP). Alternatively, you may be able to drive with a translated version of your license, depending on the country it was issued in. For longer stays, you will need to apply for a Japanese driver's license.

How old do I need to be to rent a car?

To rent a car in Japan, you generally need to be **at least 18 years old**. However, many rental companies may require drivers to be at least 21 and have held their driver's license for more than a year. Some companies may also charge an additional fee for drivers under 25. *For more details, see Chapter 18.*

Nude Beaches & Clothing-Optional Resorts

Is public nudity legal on the beaches?

No. Public nudity is **illegal** on beaches in Japan. Swimwear is required, and nudity is not tolerated. Exceptions exist in certain private areas like onsens, but public nudity can lead to fines or legal issues. *For more details, see Chapter 19.*

Tourist Taxation

Is there room tax in Japan?

Yes. Japan imposes a room tax, known as the "accommodation tax," which varies by city. This tax is charged to guests staying in hotels, inns, and other accommodations, with rates typically ranging from ¥100 to ¥500 (approximately US$0.68 to $3.40) per person per night.

Is there any fee associated with leaving Japan?

> **No.** There is no specific fee for leaving Japan, but international departure fees are typically included in the price of airline tickets. *For more details, see Chapter 22.*

Long-Term Stays

Do I need to return to my home country to apply for a work permit in Japan?

> **No.** As an American, you do not need to return to your home country to apply for a work permit in Japan. You can apply for a work visa from within Japan if you are already in the country under a temporary visitor status. However, if you are not in Japan, you will need to apply for the visa at a Japanese embassy or consulate in your home country or a third country.

As an American, how long can I stay in Japan without a visa?

> American citizens can stay in Japan for up to 90 days without a visa under the visa-exemption program for tourism, business, or short visits. If you plan to stay longer or engage in activities like work or study, you will need to apply for an appropriate visa. *For more details, see Chapter 23.*

In the Event of Death

What documents would an embassy need regarding the death of a tourist?

> If a tourist dies in Japan, the embassy will need the death certificate, the tourist's passport, a medical report on the cause of death, and possibly a police report. They may also require proof of relationship, such as a marriage or birth certificate. Once these documents are provided, the embassy can help arrange the repatriation of the body and assist with legal procedures. *For more details, see Chapter 25.*

EMERGENCY/IMPORTANT CONTACT NUMBERS IN JAPAN

 Please consider putting some of these numbers in your phone prior to traveling to Japan.

Emergency Numbers:

- **Police:** 110
- **Fire:** 119
- **Ambulance:** 119

Other Useful Contacts:

- **General Emergency Services:** 171
- **Tourist Police:** 03-3501-0110
- **Coast Guard:** 118
- **Roadside Assistance (Japan Automobile Federation):** 0570-00-8139

Legal Assistance:

- **Japan Federation of Bar Associations:** 03 -3580-9741
- **Japan Legal Support Center:** 0570-07-8377

USEFUL JAPANESE PHRASES

Greetings

HI/HELLO – こんにちは (Konnichiwa)

GOOD MORNING – おはようございます (Ohayou gozaimasu)

GOOD AFTERNOON – こんにちは (Konnichiwa)

GOOD NIGHT – おやすみなさい (Oyasuminasai)

GOODBYE – さようなら (Sayounara)

Magic Words

PLEASE – お願いします (Onegaishimasu)

THANK YOU – ありがとう (Arigatou)

YOU'RE WELCOME – どういたしまして (Dou itashimashite)

CHEERS! – 乾杯! (Kanpai)

EXCUSE ME – すみません (Sumimasen)

Getting Around

WHERE IS THE BATHROOM? – トイレはどこですか? (Toire wa doko desu ka?)

WHAT TIME IS IT? – 今、何時ですか? (Ima, nanji desu ka?)

HOW DO I GET TO...? – ...へはどう行きますか？ (... e wa dou ikimasu ka?)

WHERE DOES THIS TRAIN/BUS GO? – この電車/バスはどこへ行きますか？ (Kono densha/basu wa doko e ikimasu ka?)

RESTAURANT – レストラン (Resutoran)

HOW MUCH DOES THIS COST? – これはいくらですか？ (Kore wa ikura desu ka?)

TRAIN/METRO STATION – 駅 (Eki)

Communication

DO YOU SPEAK ENGLISH? – 英語を話せますか？ (Eigo o hanasemasu ka?)

I DO NOT UNDERSTAND – わかりません (Wakarimasen)

I DON'T SPEAK JAPANESE – 日本語が話せません (Nihongo ga hanasemasen)

I DON'T KNOW – わかりません (Wakarimasen)

Emergency

HELP! – 助けて！ (Tasukete!)

CALL AN AMBULANCE! – 救急車を呼んでください！ (Kyūkyūsha o yonde kudasai!)

I NEED A DOCTOR – 医者が必要です (Isha ga hitsuyou desu)

POLICE – 警察 (Keisatsu)

I'M LOST – 道に迷いました (Michi ni mayoimashita)

IT'S AN EMERGENCY – 緊急です (Kinkyuu desu)

GLOSSARY

ACQUITTAL: A jury verdict that a criminal defendant is not guilty, or the finding of a judge that the evidence cannot support a conviction.

ADVERSARY PROCEEDING: A lawsuit arising from a controversy that begins with filing a complaint.

AFFIDAVIT: A written statement made under oath.

APPEAL: A request made after a trial court has decided against one party in which the losing party asks a higher court to review the decision for legal error.

ARRAIGNMENT: A proceeding in which a criminal defendant is brought to court, told of the charges, and asked to plead guilty or not guilty.

BAIL: The temporary release of a person from jail when awaiting trial, on condition that a sum of money be lodged or deposited to guarantee an appearance in court.

BARRISTER: A lawyer admitted to plead at the Bar and who may try cases in superior court.

BURDEN OF PROOF: The duty to prove disputed facts.

CAUSE OF ACTION: A legal claim in a civil action.

COMPLAINT: A written statement that begins a civil lawsuit in which the plaintiff details the claims.

CONTRACT: An agreement between two or more persons to do something or to not do something.

CONVICTION: A judgment of guilt against a person charged with a crime.

CUSTOMS DUTY: A tariff or tax imposed on goods when transported across international borders.

COURT LIAISON: A person that coordinates with attorneys to perform administrative duties, such as scheduling witnesses, sharing information with law enforcement, and overseeing the reporting of cases to foreign embassies when applicable.

DAMAGES: Money that a defendant pays to a plaintiff in a civil case if the plaintiff wins.

DEFENDANT: 1) The individual against whom a civil claim is filed; 2) The individual against whom a criminal claim is filed.

FELONY: A serious crime, punishable by more than one year in prison.

MAGISTRATE: A judicial officer of a district court, who conducts initial proceedings in criminal cases, decides criminal misdemeanor cases, conducts many pretrial civil and criminal matters on behalf of district judges, and decides civil cases with the consent of the parties.

MISDEMEANOR: An offense punishable by one year or less in jail.

PLAINTIFF: A person or business that files a formal complaint with the court.

PLEA: In a criminal case, the answer of "guilty," "not guilty," or "no contest" in response to a criminal charge.

SOLICITOR: A lawyer who advises clients, represents them in lower court, and prepares cases for barristers to try in higher courts.

SOVEREIGN IMMUNITY: A legal doctrine by which the sovereign or the state (i.e. government) cannot commit a legal wrong and thus, it is immune from criminal and civil liability and cannot be sued.

STATUTE: A written law passed by a legislative body.

STATUTE OF LIMITATIONS: A statute prescribing a period of limitation to bring certain types of legal actions. If the action is not brought within that time, the person or entity (in a criminal context) is permanently barred from suing in court.

SUBPOENA: A command, issued under court authority, for a witness to appear and to give testimony.

TESTIMONY: Evidence presented orally by witnesses.

VERDICT: The decision of a judge or jury in a case.

WARRANT: Court authorization to conduct a search or to make an arrest.

ACKNOWLEDGMENTS

This book series would never have seen the light of day without the able assistance of the following people:

Kathy Adams, my paralegal for over 22 years, who is the "Best" I've ever worked with during my entire legal career because of her amazing work ethic, organizational skills, and her ability to think outside of the box in unique and creative ways;

Ally Knez-Siddique, a professional writer, and one of my paralegals, whose eye for detail, according to her, is both a blessing and a curse;

Gino Ibanez, my former law clerk, whose exceptional research skills helped move this book series along in its early stages;

Rosa Diaz Graham, my legal assistant who helped with research and word processing at the very beginning of this project;

Shelia Martin, one of my former paralegals, worked diligently on this series of books, even after taking on another job. Her organizational skills are reflected throughout;

Mindy Scarlett, my marketing and publishing "Guru"! Her creativity and vision have no boundaries!

ABOUT THE AUTHOR

Michael L. Moore practices in Orlando, Florida, the city where he spent his formative years. He credits the trauma of having his brother murdered when he was only 10 years old, as the catalyst that drew him into the practice of law.

Moore attended Florida State University, where he was a member of the FSU debate team. Upon graduating, he was awarded a full scholarship to attend the University of Tennessee College of Law, where he was elected President of the Student Bar Association. He further honed his advocacy and public speaking skills by participating in 'moot court' competitions.

After clerking at the Tennessee Attorney General's office while in law school, Moore moved back to Orlando, Florida, to work at the State Attorney's Office as a prosecutor, and where he was fortunate enough to meet the young lady that would eventually become his wife. Moore moved on to working for private law firms, both local and national, and eventually established his own law firm in 1999. He continues to make Orlando his home base.

It was the murder of a close friend and client in Jamaica that caused Moore to realize that books on laws in other countries were few and far between, and he was inspired to create Law of the Land Publishing. Moore launched Law of the Land Publishing to provide a series of guide-books and a membership site for tourists and business travelers to stay up to date on the laws in each country they travel to, as well as having access to assistance if they run into legal issues.

"My vision is to educate people on what their legal rights are, and how they can access legal assistance, no matter where they have to travel to in the world," said Moore. "As Americans, we have a right to due process, but in some countries, you don't even have the right to access a square meal when incarcerated. My goal is to provide the information needed to stay out of trouble, as well as having access to assistance if trouble finds you."

www.ingramcontent.com/pod-product-compliance
Lightning Source LLC
Chambersburg PA
CBHW070914120626
46546CB00001B/253